THE EXPERIENCE OF EMPTINESS

By

Clive Hazell

ISBN: 1-4107-9770-8 (e-book)
ISBN: 1-4107-9769-4 (Paperback)

Library of Congress Control Number: 2003097012

This book is printed on acid free paper.

Printed in the United States of America
Bloomington, IN

1stBooks - rev. 10/11/03

DEDICATION

This book is dedicated to my wife and children,
who fill my heart to overflowing.

CONTENTS

Introduction.. vii

Chapter 1
THE EXPERIENCE OF EMPTINESS 1

Chapter 2
EMPTINESS AND RESISTANCE.................... 113

Chapter 3
REMORSE AND RESISTANCE...................... 141

Chapter 4
RESISTANCE TO WORKING IN THE
HERE AND NOW.. 155

Chapter 5
EMPTINESS AND THE GROUP..................... 165

Chapter 6
CLINICAL APPLICATIONS OF THE
THEORY OF POSITIVE
DISINTEGRATION.. 187

Chapter 7
THE EXPERIENCE OF EMPTINESS AND
THE USE OF DABROWSKI'S THEORY
IN COUNSELING GIFTED CLIENTS:
CLINICAL CASE EXAMPLES 203

Chapter 8
    THE HERMENEUTIC FUNCTION: F.............. 229

REFERENCES AND BIBLIOGRAPHY 249

INTRODUCTION

The experience of emptiness is, for many people, painful, so painful that they may turn to addictions, frenzied action or violence in order to block its emergence into awareness. Yet for some, under certain conditions, it represents, and can be, liberation, an opening, and an opportunity for further growth and spontaneity.

Through theoretical exposition and case examples, this book begins to integrate various branches of psychodynamic psychology, social systems theory and Dabrowski's theory of positive disintegration in an attempt to explain the various forms of this experience.

Chapter 1

THE EXPERIENCE OF EMPTINESS

INTRODUCTION

We are the hollow men
We are the stuffed men
>Leaning together
>Headpiece filled with straw. Alas!
Shape without form, shade without color,
Paralyzed force, gesture without motion.

>T.S. Eliot,
>*The Hollow Men*

We put thirty spokes together and call it a wheel;
But it is on the space where there is nothing that
>The utility of the wheel depends.
We turn clay to make a vessel;
But it is on the space where there is nothing that
>The utility of the vessel depends.

We pierce doors and windows to make a house;

And it is on these spaces where there is nothing

That the utility of the house depends.

Therefore just as we take advantage of what is, we

Should recognize the utility of what is not.

Lao-tzu,
Tao Teh Ching (Ch. XXV)

Emptiness: A Definition of the Phenomenon

The experience of emptiness is a human experience, a feeling. As such, its nature and form is difficult to capture in technical language. Its nature is perhaps best conveyed through poetry, novels, plays or the visual arts. We can, in fact, find examples of the artistic expression of the experience of emptiness in each of these art forms.

The experience of emptiness has been captured and expressed by many artists: Kafka's *The Trial*' or *The Castle*, Sartre's *La Nausee*, Camus' *L'Etranger*, any number of the works by Beckett, such as *Molloy*,

Endgame or *Waiting for Godot*; all these deal with emptiness or aspects of it.

In the visual arts we find it expressed with exquisite delicacy and precision in the work of Edward Hopper, who, in his paintings "Nighthawks," "Seven A.M. 1948," "New York Movie, 1939" and "Entering a Town" explores and even finds beauty in the experience of emptiness as it is manifested and symbolized in the American scene—in empty movie houses, bleak cityscapes, isolated individuals in hotel lobbies and 3 A.M. diners.

Emptiness is also found in the flat, motionless images of Seurat (Un Apres-midi sur la Grande Jatte). Emptiness in a more frightening form is conveyed magnificently through the painting "The Subway," by George Tooker, 1950.

Leilah, (all names are fictional) a woman in her late thirties, described the experience as follows:

> ...I have completely lost the sense that I am master of my own ship. It's like a ship floating in the water out of control

and it's out of sight of land and its steering mechanism is spinning wildly, and I as captain have no idea of what to do and…dread is the word.

Interviewer: That's related to this feeling of emptiness?

Leilah: Right. What comes to my mind is a time when I really felt that…when I was an adolescent, I would say, late sixteen to seventeen years old when I felt like I was being asked to do all sorts of grown up things, like the main thing was go away to college and I felt like I was sort of made of paper and the inside of me was hollow and when I stood up to do things I could crumble—it was very clear that I would crumble because I was empty—and I felt hollow.

I also felt unsupported—nothing within my own self could support me and I didn't have any kind of support, moorings within my family...or feel that they could help me in any way. I didn't feel that I had them and they didn't have me. So I was set adrift in adulthood and the whole idea of going to college was like drifting into a million novel experiences and a host of adult pressures with no way of holding myself together. I think the sort of ultimate fear in that is that I will just disappear into the void.

Jane, another woman in her early forties, described the experience of emptiness as it arose with the loss of her husband through divorce:

Jane: Well I haven't felt this emptiness for a long, long time, I should say, maybe a year ago. But I remember, right after the divorce from Bill, after being married for thirteen years, I felt it a number of times, just devastatingly. I was terrified of the feeling and it's hard to describe you know—there's this feeling of emptiness in my belly—this empty feeling in the pit of my belly, and the feelings kind of radiated through my body and I felt bad, bad, bad, bad. I felt that something awful was going to happen, there's a non-existence there.

Another subject, "T," a male in his mid thirties, describes an experience of emptiness that has a distinctive "existential" ring to it since it is so redolent with a concern for authenticity:

T: Another experience of void was that there was nothing inside of me. The my personal life had been for a long time, was putting up facades, defending against what was really inside, trying to put together a façade in such a way that I could control not only the way I was, but also the behavior of others. And I guess an awful lot of energy went into that. And from time to time I would be put in positions where I would start exploring who I really was and I would try and let go of some of the facades I was holding up and the experience was (said in a whisper) "That there's nothing under there!" and it was scary, really scary.

These individuals give us an idea, often through the use of images, of what it is like to experience emptiness, they also point us towards some of the situations that might bring about the experience of emptiness, such as sudden loss, novel situations or self- exploration. Comparing these descriptions of the experience of emptiness also suggests that emptiness can be experienced in a variety of forms. Forms of feeling, as Langer (1967) points out are most precisely depicted through artistic expression. However, given the limitations of technical language in conveying the form of the feeling, what is the experience of emptiness like? I hope to demonstrate that it is a separate, discrete feeling-state, close to some other, more commonly recognized feeling-states, yet possessing important and telling differences from these.

For example, emptiness is sometimes close to boredom in that there is commonly associated a debilitating lack of interest in one's environment and a lassitude or a lack of enthusiasm. The difference from the experience of emptiness is that emptiness is diffuse and not focused on specific experiences. Boredom is often directed at an object or experience and can easily develop into angry rejection of that experience. In the experience of emptiness, no such clarity or feeling is present. It is a vague and nebulous malaise that seems to seep into every fiber of one's existence, robbing it of purpose, meaning, hope and, ultimately, experience itself.

Emptiness can sometimes be close to the experience of futility or helplessness. It is different, however, in that in these feeling states, there is the clear experience of something having been lost. This feeling of loss is absent in the experience of emptiness.

With this experience, nothing was possessed, nothing lost and nothing is to be gained. The emptiness or numbness is a miasma that seeps forward and backward along time. Memories and anticipations lose all affective charge. Consequently, motivation and choice are encountered "avec une grande indifference."

With hopelessness, for example, the barren psychological landscape extends largely into the future and not so extensively into the past; for if there is hopelessness, there must once have been hope, however fleeting and vaporous, and a belief in the possibility of capturing the good object or experience.

Emptiness is a paradoxical feeling state. It is painful. To experience emptiness, especially chronically, is to endure misery. Its keynote, however, is that the feelings normally associated with misery—sadness, loneliness, longing, hopelessness, despair—are missing. The person may introspectively seek these feelings inside him/herself, but he/she just draws a blank. Very often, for the person experiencing emptiness, to cry, to feel lonely, or to weep in despair can be, paradoxically, a relief—a release from the burden of non-feeling into the reality, albeit a painful reality, of being a feeling human. At times, however, the contact with the feeling may be too overwhelming and the experience of emptiness, by comparison, is soothing in its very blandness. In this case, the emptiness continues as a chronic feeling state for the individual.

Emptiness is not the same as loneliness although people who experience it may feel extremely isolated—often by virtue of the experience of emptiness itself. Loneliness involves a desire to be with others—a longing for human contact. This feeling, painful though it may be, provides an orientation of the individual and thus some sense of "self-feeling" (Jacobson, 1964). The experience of emptiness cannot co-exist with the feeling of loneliness, for with loneliness, the individual still, on some level, maintains the belief that there is or was someone "out there" for him or her. With the experience of emptiness it is as if the internal representations of these desirable entities or experiences have been obliterated, leaving the person with no substantial experience of what they are missing or what they want.

Forms of nihilistic or iconoclastic rage are not in themselves emptiness, although they may betoken its subterranean existence. In nihilistic rage, there is the clear presence of emotion, and entities that once were valued are now destroyed as if meaningless. Once the rage has played itself out, the experience may be that of emptiness, for there may be no internal trace of a desirable goal and the intense feelings of loss, guilt and reparation engendered by the destructiveness may be locked away in a psychological oubliette, unavailable to conscious scrutiny and thus engendering the lack of experienced emotion characteristic of emptiness. It is interesting to posit, in passing, that societies and groups may go through similar processes after outbursts of rage that have iconoclastic import such as wars or revolutions.

The individual who experiences emptiness may never experience loneliness, may be puzzled by others' experiences of loneliness or may from time to time, long for, in an estranged fashion, the experience for him or herself.

However, emptiness can apparently take on different forms. So far the descriptions of emptiness have been of what might be termed "pure emptiness," or "blankness." Another form of emptiness has been construed, however. This other form is called "Existential emptiness." In this feeling-state, the feelings of inner numbness or void are combined with a heightened concern over specific existential issues: death, authenticity and the meaning of life. Frankl has written extensively on this topic (1958, 1965, 1967) stating that is constitutes a symptom of the "Existential neurosis."

In general, psychoanalytic writers (Kernberg, Kohut) write about the "pure emptiness," unadorned with existential concerns. The existential psychologists ostensibly focus on existential emptiness but include in their definition experiences that do not have specific existential content, as defined here. One of my aims is to demonstrate that Frankl's concept of existential emptiness is comprised of two factors:

existential concern and emptiness; that not all emptiness is existential emptiness and existential concern does not necessarily imply emptiness. I also intend to demonstrate that the psychoanalytic concept of emptiness is not all-inclusive.

Various forms of emptiness are therefore hypothesized to exist depending on the admixture of these two components, existential concern and experienced level of emptiness. These various forms of the experience of emptiness are in turn hypothesized to be dependent not only upon the factors mentioned in the literature, but also upon certain specific personality traits, situational and developmental characteristics of the individual.

Why Study Emptiness?

In addition to a need for conceptual clarity, there are practical reasons for doing this study. If, as May (1953) suggests, the experience of emptiness is almost as common as lower back pain in this society, further understanding of this phenomenon might lead to some alleviation of suffering. Following are some potential benefits that might accrue from a study in this area:

(a) The suicide rate is hypothesized to be strongly related to emptiness. An understanding of the conditions that rob life of meaning and make the person feel empty would throw light on this important area.

(b) The experience of emptiness and existential vacuum is, probably, quite common. It is at the same time an experience that is rarely spoken of or recognized either interpersonally or in the day-to-day process of institutions. Some further understanding of a widespread and growing phenomenon would seem to be of value.

(c) There are certain types of behavior hypothesized to be associated with certain forms of existential vacuum. Frankl (1963, pp. 169-172) asserts that various forms of "acting out" behavior occur in reaction to the experience of existential vacuum. May (1950, p. 182) believes that the loss of the sense of self that is associated with the related concept of existential anxiety causes the person to seek some strong and distinct feelings in order to shore up the disintegrating sense of self. This quest for strong feelings can involve activity that does harm to both self and others, e.g. vandalism, eating disorders, delinquency, compulsive sexuality, addiction.

In addition, certain psychoanalytically-oriented writers such as Kohut (1971, 1977), Bruch (1973, 1979) and Kernberg (1975, 1976) posit strong causal relationships between the experience of emptiness and various forms of "acting out" behavior.

Hopefully, this book will lead to some insights into the nature of the experience of emptiness and will begin to provide a conceptual framework to understand this experience in the different forms it takes. Clinicians will hopefully be better able to predict, understand and empathize with the many individuals whom they see presenting with this complaint.

To experience emptiness chronically is to be out of touch with one's vitality and one's feelings on a long-term basis. Living in this fashion, given the ultimate importance of feelings in providing orientation in personal and social space, is like embarking on a polar expedition, blindfolded and with no maps. Living in the absence of such valuable orientation may, over an expanse of many years, expose the individual to chronically harmful conditions which are sustained simply because the emotional information about the harmful nature of the situation is not available owing to inner numbness or emptiness. Thus the chronic experience of emptiness may indirectly render the person, unaware, vulnerable to stress and breakdown diseases. In other words, emptiness may work in a fashion analogous to, say, hypertension, in the somatic domain. Hypertension is essentially a symptom-free condition. That is to say, it may not manifest itself in the realm of behavior or perceptible concrete occurrence. Left untreated, however, it renders the individual extremely vulnerable to cardio-vascular disease. In the same way, emptiness may not manifest itself except through a narrow form of measurement or in the therapy situation, but its psychosomatic ravages continue, unchecked, beneath the surface of casual observation, until the tragic results become manifest in the personal or the social field in the form of self-destruction.

Review of the Literature and Theoretical Foundations

Freedom exists and the will also exists; but freedom of the will does not exist, for a will that is directed towards its own freedom thrusts into emptiness.

Thomas Mann,
Mario and the Magician

To me the Universe was void of all Life, of Purpose, of Volition, even of Hostility: it was one huge dead, immeasurable steam engine, rolling on, in its dead indifference, to grind me limb from limb.

Thomas Carlyle,
Sartor Resartus

Introduction

The experience of emptiness has been written about by five categories of thinkers: artists, such as Tolstoy (1868), Hemingway (1933), Kafka (1925, 1926, 1927), Dostoievsky (1861, 1864); theologians, such as Tillich (1952), Suzuki (1956), Streng (1967); philosophers, such as Sartre (1956), Camus (1965);

psychoanalysts, such as Kohut (1971, 1975), Kernberg (1975, 1976) and existential psychologists such as May (1950, 1953) and Frankl (1948, 1967). It has not been examined specifically by psychologists of a more psychometric or experimental orientation. This research hopes to begin to fill that void.

In this section, I hope to set the intellectual stage for later sections by explicating and reviewing some of the major contributions in this field of the experience of emptiness and by outlining the theoretical groundwork upon which this study is based.

Existential Philosophy and the Experience of Emptiness

Jean-Paul Sartre

The experience of emptiness is discussed at some length by a number of existentialist philosophers. Of note among these writers is Sartre, whose *L'Etre et Le Neant* (1957) explores this experience in considerable detail. Many of Sartre's ideas prove tantalizing indeed when juxtaposed with ideas on the experience of emptiness that hail from analytic and developmental literature.

Among the many writers on Sartre, perhaps one of the most cogent and coherent is Warnock, whose work *The Philosophy of Sartre* (1965) provides an accessible inroad to his thought.

For Sartre, the experience of emptiness is an essential component of consciousness, freedom, and choice, all of which, in his philosophical system, are closely related. If human beings become conscious or self-aware, that is, if they reflect upon themselves, they of necessity create a "gap" between observer and observed.

> "...knowledge entails that the object known is held at a distance from the person who knows it: he distinguishes the object from himself and thereby forms the judgment, "I am not the object." This distance at which the object is held is the gap or nothingness of the "for-itself."
>
> (Warnock, 1965, p.61)

This gap is experienced as a void or nothingness in the self. The same process occurs, argues Sartre, when a person has a "project" or a plan. In having a plan, a person becomes aware to some degree of the gap between what is and what can be. Again, this gap is experienced as an inner emptiness. This emptiness is very close to the experience of "anguish" which, Sartre, contends, is part and parcel of the experience of freedom, or of exercising choice, and of taking responsibility for one's actions. It is this emptiness from which humans tend to recoil in acts of what Sartre calls "mauvaise foi" or "bad faith." The two major forms of bad faith are "being-for-others" which means playing roles to meet others' expectations, or turning oneself into a thing or an inanimate object.

Sartre posits that another alternative in this situation is to face the "nothingness in the center of consciousness" and make conscious choices. In *The Critique of Dialectical Reason* (1964) he writes:

> Freedom is precisely the nothingness which is made to be in the heart of man.
> (Sartre, 1964)

Sartre thus not only sees the experience of inner void as something that is immanent in man but that is also inextricably linked with the exercising of consciousness and freedom:

> Without the gap or vacancy within them, conscious beings would become unconscious beings—in-themselves, wholly determined by being whatever they are—conscious beings have no essences. Instead of an essential core they have nothing.
> (Warnock, 1965, p. 62)

However, bad faith, or the numbing of ourselves against consciousness, freedom and choice is inevitable in the course of human life and this tendency is counterbalanced by the inevitability of inner nothingness with consciousness.

> But if all conscious beings are necessarily separated from their future actions and their vision of themselves

> by a gap. If consciousness actually
> consists in the presence of this
> emptiness which has to be filled by free
> thoughts and choices, then plainly we
> cannot avoid Bad Faith altogether. We
> may aspire to be whatever we are
> completely, but we can never achieve
> this. We cannot become "massif," like
> inkwells, as long as we remain
> conscious.
>
> (Sartre, 1964)

There are many linkages between the work of Sartre on the experience of nothingness and certain areas of developmental and psychodynamic psychology.

First, if it can be assumed that consciousness and self-reflection increase with age in the early years of life, as an aspect of psychological development, then we might expect that the experience of emptiness might be linked with this in some ways—increasing, for example during the period of acquisition of "formal operations" (Piaget, 1976). Or, as Hazell (1984a, 1984b, 1989) has suggested, there may exist a relationship between the level of experience of emptiness and the level of emotional development.

Second, there may be a linkage between the experience of emptiness/nothingness and the process of separation/individuation (Mahler, 1975). The distancing of self and object (Jacobson, 1964; Hoffer, 1951) and the capacity to arrive at the statement, "I am not the object" (Warnock, 1965, p. 61) clearly implies a process of separation/ individuation. Further research would be necessary to elucidate the nature of this connection, if it does in fact exist.

At the root of such cross-paradigmatic comparisons and linkages lies a semantic issue. Is the experience of nothingness that Sartre describes the same as the experience of emptiness described by writers in other paradigms? Herein lies a serious problem that hampers further study in this area. In another study I attempted some small step in the area of operationalizing the concept of emptiness to facilitate any further meaningful discussion in this arena (Hazell 1984b, 1989)

Sartre, of course, is not the only existential philosopher to discuss the experience of nothingness. Heidegger (1927) before him and Kierkegaard (1843) have dilated upon this topic in their own fashion. And while there are many divergences of opinion and explanation for the experience of emptiness or nothingness in the various sub-schools of existentialism, there are some tantalizingly fertile linkages, that, if explored, may help to elucidate this area of human experience.

Theology and the Experience of Emptiness

Paul Tillich

Tillich (1952) approaches the experience of emptiness from the viewpoint of Christian existentialism. Tillich takes as his starting point the experience of anxiety. Generally, he denies anxiety as the result of a threat to the individual's self-affirmation. It is a threat of non-being.

> Non-being is omnipresent and produces anxiety even where an immediate Threat of death is absent
> > (Tillich, 1952, p. 45)

Tillich argues that there are three basic types of anxiety, each corresponding to three sectors of human consciousness: First is the anxiety of "Fate and Death" which results from the threat of man's ontic self-affirmation. ("*Ontos*" is the Greek word for "being"). Secondly, there is the anxiety of "Emptiness and Meaninglessness," which is occasioned by an assault on man's spiritual being.

The anxiety of emptiness and meaninglessness is brought on, Tillich argues, by the destruction of the human's capacity to be "spiritually creative" (Tillich, 1952).

> Spiritual affirmation occurs in every moment in which man lives creatively in the various spheres of meaning…In order to be spiritually creative one need not be what is called a creative artist or scientist or statesman, but one must be able to participate meaningfully in their original creations.
>
> (Tillich, 1953)

And, further delineating the natural history of the experience and some of its possible causes, he states:

> The anxiety of emptiness is aroused by the threat of nonbeing to the special contents of the spiritual life. A belief breaks down through external events or inner processes: one is cut off from creative participation in a sphere of culture, one feels frustrated about something which one had passionately affirmed, one is driven from devotion to one object to another and again on to another, because the meaning of each of them vanishes and the creative eros is transformed into indifference or aversion. Everything is tried and nothing satisfies. The contents of the tradition, however excellent, however praised, however loved once, lose their power to give content today. And present culture is even less able to provide the content. Anxiously one turns away from all concrete contents and looks for an ultimate meaning, only to discover that it was precisely the loss of a spiritual center which took away the meaning of the special contents of the spiritual life. But a spiritual center cannot be produced intentionally and

> the attempt to produce it only produces deeper anxiety. The anxiety of emptiness drives us to the abyss of meaningless.
>
> (Tillich, 1953, p. 48)

Tillich argues that the response to this fear is indeed risky, for it is likely that, in the absence of an internal source of meaning, the individual, deep in the clutch of this form of anxiety, will turn to external sources of meaning. This has the effect of preserving his sense of meaning, but sacrificing his true self. This, Tillich argues, is at the root of fanaticism. It is the phenomenon of "the escape from freedom" that Fromm (1955) speaks of. It is thus conceivable that there are individuals who avoid their inner emptiness through adapting to authoritarianism, engaging in primitive forms of hero-worship, and sacrificing their individuality in mindless conformity.

Tillich believes that the participation of the individual in meaningful systems of symbols is vital to self-affirmation and to an avoidance, in a salutary fashion, of the anxiety of emptiness. Very often this participation requires a special form of courage.

Tillich calls this "The Courage to Be" or "The Courage to Be as Part." Tillich does not underestimate the courage it might take, for the threat to one's spiritual affirmation ultimately resounds through the other sectors of self-affirmation—moral and ontic: "The most revealing expression of this fact is the desire to throw away one's ontic existence rather than stand the despair of emptiness and meaningless."

A corollary to this thesis is that threats in the ontic and moral sectors of man's self-affirmation will result in an undermining of the spiritual self-affirmation. In other words, the sense of meaning will be lost when there is a rude threat to existence or when one has transgressed a precious moral code.

Tillich's work has been influential in the field of counseling in general and existential psychology in particular. One may note many parallels between his thought and the other schools of thought represented here.

It may be of value to note in passing that the experience of emptiness is a central experience in the religion of Zen Buddhism where it is called the "satori" (Suzuki, 1956; Streng, 1967). This form of emptiness is indeed fascinating and does find itself described in the works of Western psychologists (Perls, 1969, 1973).

The form of emptiness that we encounter in the thought and art of Zen, and the "fertile void" of which Perls (1969) speaks is a form of experience where the individual momentarily is able to perceive him or herself and the world around in a fresh manner, unfettered by rubric, preconception or stereotypy. It is something of a "transcendent" experience since it supervenes, in an often shocking manner, one's usual way of experiencing things. It can be said to be close to the experiences of creative perceiving that are to be found in the theory of Schactel (1959).

These forms of emptiness are perhaps of a different order from the concept of blank emptiness or existential emptiness. I believe they are the form of emptiness found at higher levels of emotional development. More of this later.

Existential Psychologies and The Experience of Emptiness

Viktor Frankl

Frankl has coined the term "Existential vacuum" (1975) and aspects of the meaning of this term come close in meaning to the term "emptiness" as it is defined in this study. Frankl posits that humans have a "will to meaning" which is as basic to them as the will to power or the will to pleasure of Nietzsche and Freud, respectively. The frustration of the will to meaning results, in Frankl's estimation, in a "noogenic neurosis"—an abyss experience.

Frankl thinks that the extent of these complaints is quite wide: As to the existential vacuum, however…

> A statistical survey recently showed that among my European students, 25% had this experience…
> Among my American students, it was not 25% but 50%.
> (Frankl, 1975)

Frankl identifies three major "failures" that lead to the experience of existential vacuum: a failure in responsibility, a failure in faith and a failure in appreciating the whole being. In this, Frankl seems to be in harmony with the thinking of May (1953) who feels that one of the major causes of the experience of emptiness is the "alienation" that is present in modern society.

In Frankl's thinking, the experience of emptiness is comprised of two feelings:

a. A feeling that life is meaningless.
b. A feeling of inner emptiness.

Frankl appears to appreciate a bifactorial quality in the experience of existential vacuum, but in other places the term existential vacuum is undifferentiated from other concepts such as boredom and depression. For example:

> "This existential vacuum manifests itself mainly in a state of boredom."
> (Frankl, 1963, p. 169)

On the same page, he states that the existential vacuum is a form of "Sunday Neurosis"—"that kind of depression which afflicts those who become aware of the lack of content in their lives when the rush of the busy week is over and the void within themselves becomes manifest." (Frankl, 1963, p. 169)

Frankl thus leaves the definition of existential vacuum in a fairly diffuse form and unconnected to any developmental theory. While Freud, for example, relates the will to pleasure to the development of the individual, no such attempt of relating the will to meaning to human development is made by Frankl.

Conceptually, Frankl's work stands at the boundary of philosophy and the psychology of the introspectionists.

Rollo May

May writes most extensively about the experience of emptiness in his book, *Man's Search for Himself* (1953). Here he manifests a clearly existentially influenced viewpoint, echoing the thoughts found in his earlier work, *The Meaning of*

Anxiety, (1950). This is perhaps related to the fact that May was a student of Tillich.

In his earlier work, May (1950) connects the experience of anxiety with the threat of nonbeing: Anxiety is the experience of being affirming itself against nonbeing (May, 1950, p. xxi).

Here, May echoes the thoughts of existentialist philosophy, especially that of Kierkegaard. "Emptiness and loneliness," asserts May, "are thus the two phases of the basic experience of anxiety." May believes that the problem of the experience of emptiness is quite widespread.

> …the chief problem of problem in the mid-decade of the twentieth century is emptiness. By that I mean that not only do people not know what they want; they often do not have any clear idea of what they feel…they have no definite experience of their desires or wants.
>
> (May, 1953, p. 14).

And, anticipating Kohut (1977) in noting a shift from "Guilty man" to "Tragic man," May notes:

> …the most common problem now is not social taboos on sexual activity or guilt feelings about sex itself, but the fact that sex for most people is an empty, mechanical and vacuous experience.
>
> (May, 1953, p.15).

May picks up on the theme of "other-directedness," citing David Reisman's book, *The Lonely Crowd*. "People," May argues, "know what they should want but not what they really want," and they are thus trapped into empty conformity. But, May argues, this conformity is fragile, at best:

> People who live as "hollow men" can endure the monotony only by an occasional blow-off, or at least by identifying with someone else's blow-off.
>
> (May, 1953, p. 20).

May also connects the experience of emptiness, or reactions to it, to drug addiction, where the individual, lacking a clear internal sense of self, attempts to create an ersatz experience in order to fill the void pharmacologically.

May thinks that the causes of the increased experience of emptiness lie in the social and psychological changes that have taken place in the twentieth century.

The upheaval of societies' values gives us no idea of "what we are and what we ought to be," as Matthew Arnold puts it (May, 1953).

Thus, one could argue that May sees the experience of emptiness as the individual, personal experience that arises out of the social condition of anomie.

This connection is further delineated as May attempts to correlate the experience of emptiness, helplessness and powerlessness.

The experience of emptiness, rather, generally comes from people's feeling that they are powerless to do anything effective about their lives or the world they live in. Inner vacuousness is the long-term accumulated result of a person's particular conviction towards himself, namely, that he cannot act as an entity in directing his own life...and soon since what he wants and what he feels can make no real difference, he gives up wanting and feeling. Apathy and lack of feeling are also defenses against anxiety (May, 1953, p. 22).

May goes further to point out some grave dangers that lie ahead for a society whose members are experiencing emptiness:

> Its end results are the dwarfing and impoverishing of persons psychologically, or else surrender to some destructive authoritarianism.
> (May, 1953, p. 23)

Thus May makes the important connection between this cycle of events: helplessness-apathy-emptiness-authoritarianism. The experience thus is a log that may fuel the fires of certain harmful social systems, political and organizational structures.

Psychoanalytic Thought and the Experience of Emptiness

Otto Kernberg

Kernberg (1975) devotes an entire chapter to an examination of the experience of emptiness. He uses psychodynamics and object-relations theory as a means of explaining the various forms the experience might take. For Kernberg, the experience of emptiness arises when there is a loss of what Jacobson (1964) calls "self-feeling." He points out that although there are several forms of the experience of emptiness, there are two broad reactions to the experience: that of "acting out" in a forced attempt to regain a sense of internal aliveness, and that of submitting to the experience and going through one's daily activities in a split-off, mechanical fashion.

Kernberg describes the feeling of emptiness as it may occur in four personality types, arguing that its form, intensity and etiology will differ in each type.

In a person suffering from chronic neurotic depression, the emptiness, he states, is caused by a primitive superego that destroys the internal objects of the person.

> The harsh internal punishment inflicted by the superego consists in the implicit dictum that they do not deserve to be loved and appreciated and that they are condemned to be alone.
>
> (Kernberg, 1974, p. 215)

Kernberg differentiates this sense of emptiness from loneliness in that, "loneliness implies elements of longing and the sense that there are others that are needed, and whose love is needed and who seem unavailable now." If this longing were present, the individual would not feel empty. Emptiness is the lack of others without the realization of the lack or the longing to fill the lack.

The experience of emptiness is different for schizoid individual. These individuals may experience emptiness as an innate quality that makes them different from other people:

> ...in contrast to others, they cannot feel anything and they may feel guilty because they do not have available feelings of love, hatred, tenderness, longing or mourning which they observe and understand in other people but feel unavailable to experience themselves.
>
> (Kernberg, 1975, p. 215)

The experience of emptiness may be less painful for the person with a schizoid personality structure than the depressed individual. There is less contrast between periods of emptiness and other times and these persons are able, through an inner sense of unreality to soothe themselves and form passive-dependent relations on others which help him or her focus on the environment rather than on their subjective experience. The person with the schizoid personality structure experiences emptiness largely as a result of defensive dispersal, splitting and fragmentation of feelings. They thus feel an internal vagueness—drifting, and without orientation.

Patients with narcissistic personality structures are also very prone to the experience of emptiness. In contrast to the depressive or schizoid patients mentioned before, these narcissistic patients' experiences of emptiness are characterized by the addition of strong feelings of boredom and restlessness.

Patients with depressive personality and even schizoid patients, are able to empathize deeply with human feelings and experiences involving other people, and may feel painfully excluded from and yet able to empathize with love and emotion involving others...patients with narcissistic personality, on the other hand, do not have that capacity for empathizing with human experience in depth. Their social life, which gives them opportunities to obtain confirmation in reality or fantasy of their needs to be admired, and offers them direct instinctual gratifications, may provide them with an immediate sense of meaningfulness, but this is temporary. When such gratifications are not forthcoming, their sense of emptiness, restlessness and boredom take over. Now their world becomes a prison from which only new excitement, admiration, or experiences implying control, triumph or incorporation of supplies are an escape. Emotional reactions in depth to art, the investment in value systems or in creativity beyond gratification of their narcissistic aims is often unavailable and indeed strange to them.

(Kernberg, 1975, p. 218)

Kernberg points out that the experience of emptiness will occur in many borderline cases, but not with the pervasiveness found in narcissistic or schizoid structures.

In paranoid patients, he asserts, one will often find that the engagement with the persecutor and potential enemies is a protection against the painful experience of emptiness.

In general Kernberg posits that:

> The experience of emptiness represents a temporary or permanent loss of the normal relationship of the self with the object relations, that is, with the world of inner objects that fixates intrapsychically the significant experiences with others and constitutes a basic ingredient of ego-identity... Therefore all patients with the syndrome of identity diffusion (but not with identity crises) present the potential for developing experiences of emptiness.
>
> (Kernberg, 1975, p. 220).

Kernberg, along with Keniston (1968) believes that the experience of emptiness grows not so much out of cultural changes such as are seen in the "age of alienation," but more out of early childhood conflicts and family pathology. The rapid changes of society only bring about experiences of emptiness it there exists severe pathology of internalized object relations which stem from infancy and early childhood.

Clearly, Kernberg's paradigm for explaining the experience of emptiness is very different from Sartre's explication of "le neant." It is not even clear that they are discussing the same experience. The individual seeking an explanation for this experience is faced with a veritable panoply of varied disquisitions. He or she is faced with a knotty choice between paradigms, confounded by an absence of an operational definition.

In a passing attempt to draw some of these theories together, we may note that there exist some similarities between the depressive and schizoid types of Kernberg and what is called Level Three in the theory of emotional development (see pages 52-59) and that Kernberg's description of narcissistic personality fits quite neatly the depiction of Level One of emotional development given by Dabrowski and Piechowski (1977). The forms of emptiness described by Zen masters would correspond to Level Four of Dabrowski's system.

Masterson (1972), to a great extent following the lead of Kernberg (1975), Fairbairn and Mahler (1975), claims that the experience of "void" is one of the essential symptoms of the borderline patient. Masterson describes the experience as follows and offers a brief explanation of its etiology:

> The sense of void is best described as a terrifying inner emptiness or numbness; it springs partially from introjection of mother's negative attitudes that leaves the patients devoid, or empty of positive supportive introjects (1972, p.61).

Masterson furthermore believes that the sense of emptiness, which is part and parcel of the "borderline personality disorder," results from a breakdown in the "rapprochement" phase of the separation/individuation process as outlined by Mahler (1975).

Heinz Kohut

In describing and explaining the subjective experience of emptiness (Kohut (1971, 1977)) takes a different tack from Kernberg. While Kernberg interprets the experience largely in term of object relations, occasionally resorting to more traditional psychodynamic thinking, Kohut uses the framework of "self psychology" to explain this experience. He states:

> The psychology of the self is needed to explain the pathology of the fragmented self and of the depleted self (empty depression; i.e. the world of unmirrored ambitions, the world devoid of ideals) —in short, the psychic disturbances and struggles of "Tragic Man."
> (Kohut, 1977, p. 243)

Thus, the subjective experience of emptiness arises owing to fissures or lacunae in the mental structure that Kohut calls the self.

Thus, in describing a patient who suffered from chronic diffuse experiences of emptiness, Kohut writes:

> He suffered from a serious disturbance of his self-esteem and a deep sense of inner emptiness, a manifestation of his primary structural defect—chronic enfeeblement of his self with some tendency toward the temporary fragmentation of this structure.
>
> (Kohut, 197, p. 6)

Kohut argues that the experience of emptiness is a symptom of the narcissistic personality disorders. These are personality disorders that arise from a breakdown of the person's self-esteem and ambitions. They are caused by inadequate empathic "mirroring" and the traumatic (i.e. sub-optimal) disillusionment in idealized figures in the child's early life, and the absence of the self-objectal experience of "twinning."

According to Kohut, the self structure (self representation) matures gradually in response to optimal failures in mirroring and in idealized figures. If the failures are sub-optimal, the self-structure becomes friable and labile. One of the experiential outcroppings of this is the experience of emptiness, especially ion the face of criticism or lack of warmth or acclaim from the environment. Kohut argues that very often, in response to the early traumatic environmental failures, there develop reactions, very often in the way of soothing mechanism, to cope with and alleviate the pain of the inner emptiness.

On occasion, the person will develop "a psychic surface that is out of contact with an active nuclear self" (Kohut, 1977, p. 49). This concept sounds extremely close to the concept of "False self system" as forwarded by Winnicott (1965) and developed by Laing (1969). The false self is like a mask or a set of clothes, donned to adapt to society but cut of from the individual's real self which lies hidden, even to the individuals themselves. This psychological state can lead to frequent experiences of emptiness since when the person attempts to discover their "true feelings" they are so alienated from them through habit that they draw a blank and feel empty. Kohut, along with all those in the psychodynamic school relate this state of affairs to the early infantile environment especially the holding and handling environment of the infant. (It is interesting to note in passing the similarities between the terrain being covered here and Sartre's concept of mauvaise foi, (see p. 18) and the concept of other-directedness that Reisman describes in *The Lonely Crowd.*

Among the symptomatic responses to the experience of emptiness, Kohut cites the following: an excessive interest in words, pseudovitality, compulsive sexuality, addictions, and delinquency. Each of these, claims Kohut, are reactions to the inner experience of emptiness and are employed as means of counteracting the experience in some way.

Kohut also posits that young adulthood and middle age the critical testing grounds for the cohesiveness of the sense of self and are thus times when the individual is especially prone to experience of emptiness. Kohut also believes that this era in history is the era of the endangered self, echoing some of May's statements on this topic. Kohut further posits:

> The work of great artists,…reflects the dominant psychological issue of his era…it is the crumbling decomposing, fragmenting, enfeebling self of this child and later the fragile, vulnerable and empty self of the adult that the great artists of the day describe…that they try to heal.
>
> (Kohut, 1977, pp. 285-286)

Hilde Bruch

Bruch (1973, 1979) proffers some tantalizing observations with regard to the experience of emptiness in eating disorders in general and anorexia nervosa in particular. A nineteen year-old anorexic, for example, when asked for the reasoning behind her eating disorder, states: "I wanted to avoid anxiety, emptiness, disconnectedness, suffering" (Bruch, 1979, p. 75).

Bruch makes observations that seem to echo Kohut (1971, 1977) and others, when she reports the following person's feelings:

> Like other anorexics she was troubled by feelings of emptiness, not knowing

> what role to play, hating herself for gaining weight, but mostly by the question: "Why should anybody be like me?…what is me? When I am alone, I can't define what I am like."
>
> (Bruch, 1979, p. 152)

Further echoes are found in this report also:

> …a thirty-five years old woman who had been a binge eater for over fifteen years, used a similar image to describe the emptiness of her life that would trigger a bout of gorging…she would prepare lists, to "protect myself from something that I very frightening to me—spaces in my life"
>
> (Bruch, 1979, p. 93)

Bruch thus seems to make a connection between the self psychology and the various eating disorders in that she notes a weakened, enfeebled sense of self, a tendency towards what Sartre might call "Being-for-others" (1946) or Winnicott (1965) or Laing (1969) might call a "false self system," and chronic feelings of worthlessness and emptiness. Bruch states:

> These youngsters appear to have no conviction of their own inner substance and value and are preoccupied with satisfying the image others have of them.
>
> (Bruch, 1979, p. 45)

Or, as one anorectic patient reports:

> I felt a terrible fragmentation of myself. There wasn't a person inside me at all. I tried with whoever I was with to reflect the image they had of me.
>
> (Bruch, 1979, p. 51)

Alice Miller

The approach of Alice Miller (1981) to an explanation of the experience of emptiness falls into the psychodynamic category. For Miller, the experience of emptiness is the result of a split occurring in the person between the "real self" and the "false self." This in turn leads to an alienation from the self and an estrangement from spontaneous emotional life that is experienced by the person as emptiness.

Accommodation to parental needs often, but not always, leads to the "as-if personality" (Winnicott has described it as the "false self"). This person develops in such a way that he reveals only what is expected of him and he fuses so completely with what he reveals that—until he comes to analysis —one would scarcely have guessed how much more there is to him, behind this "masked view of himself" (Habermas, 1970). He cannot develop and differentiate his "true self" because he is unable to live it. It remains "in a state of noncommunication" as Winnicott has expressed it.

Understandably, these patients complain of a sense of emptiness, futility or hopelessness, for the emptiness is real. A process of emptying, impoverishment, and partial killing of his potential actually took place when all that was alive and spontaneous in him was cut off.
(Miller, 1981, p.12)

Miller, in a fashion similar to other psychoanalytic writers, relates the experience of emptiness to the existence of crushing negative introjects. She adds, in her analysis, the additional component of the presence or absence of spontaneous feeling as a determinant of the experienced level of emptiness. In so doing, she provides a possible conceptual link between he theorizing and this study in that the dimension of accessibility of feeling are implicitly in the theory of emotional development as is the capacity to be astonished at oneself, which is an especial feature in individuals at level three of emotional development.

And, harkening back to Kernberg and Kohut, Miller writes:

> An adult can only be fully aware of his feelings if he has internalized an affectionate and empathic self-object. People with narcissistic disturbances are missing out on this. Therefore they are never overtaken by unexpected emotions and will only admit those feelings that are accepted and approved by their inner censor, which is their parents' heir. Depression and a sense of inner emptiness is the price they must pay for this control. To return to Winnicott's concept, the true self cannot communicate because it has

remained unconscious, and therefore undeveloped, in its inner prison.

(Miller, 1981, p. 21)

Other Psychodynamically-oriented Writers

Subtle variants of these psychodynamic explanations for the experience of emptiness, basically growing out of "object relations theory," can be found in a number of other works, for example; Giovachinni (1979), Searles (1965), and Winnicott (1964, pp. 200-201).

Bowlby (1980, pp. 85-86, 153, 160) follows the thought of Winnicott in that he connects the feeling of emptiness with the experience of loss. "Numbness" and "emptiness" are, in Bowlby's model, the first phases of the human being's reaction to a loss. For Bowlby this loss is confined to a loss through death. Bowlby argues, however, that a small loss may act as a trigger for a reactivation of a prior, more serious loss.

Bowlby too offers a hint at an explanation for the feeling of emptiness or numbness, although he does not propose it as such. He cites the disruption of habitual responses that occurs for the person who has recently been bereaved. This, in turn, leads to a vague sense of disorientation, much akin to the disorientation Bowlby mentions in his earlier works on attachment and separation (Bowlby, 1980, p. 94).

Langs (1978) offers some fascinating thoughts on the experience of emptiness also. In *The Listening Process*, he posits that the experience of emptiness results from a type of "communicative field" that is essentially non-communicative:

> The Type C field is characterized by the pervasive absence of interpretable derivatives of unconscious fantasies, memories and introjects and by the presence of massive defense barriers. As a rule, the patient's communications are on a manifest content level and there is a remarkable sense of flatness and emptiness to behaviors and associations (p. 577).

Langs goes on to add:

> Type C patients typically speak from time to time of things being meaningless, of huge brick and concrete

> walls, of empty vacuums and abysses, of death and coffins and graves...(p. 579).

And according to Langs,

> Many of the narcissistic patients recently described by Kohut (1971, 1977) and Kernberg (1975) appear to function in the Type C field...(p. 611).

Thus Langs appears to link the experience of emptiness to the character structure of the individual and the type of communication he or she is likely to engage in. Langs implies that the experience of emptiness may well derive from early experiences such as those posited by other psychoanalytically-based theoreticians, and adds the interesting theoretical addition that the experience of emptiness may be precipitated by certain forms of communicative interaction.

Summary of Review of Literature

This summary has perhaps shown how the concept of the experience of emptiness has captured the attention of many writers in diverse fields. It has also shown, hopefully, the diversity of ideas and explanations related to this experience.

What stands out as clear is that the experience of emptiness is itself multiform. We may examine, for example, Kernberg's types of emptiness. One clear dimension that cuts across all the discussion of the experience of emptiness is the degree to which the emptiness is construed as an existential issue or not. For Frankl, May and Tillich, the experience of emptiness is clearly an existential emptiness. For the psychoanalytic thinkers this is not the case. The emptiness they describe is not hooked into the concept of existential concern.

A further issue concerns the immanence of the experience in humankind. For Sartre, for example, the experience of emptiness is something that is essential to man's nature. Kernberg seems to imply that this very position, namely that of accepting the experience of emptiness as something innate, is perhaps an indicator of psychopathology of the schizoid type.

Another dimension that cross-cuts and differentiates the many approaches to the experience of emptiness is the extent to which the cause of emptiness is seen as lying in the social life of humans. The existential psychologists, such as May and Frankl are perhaps the strongest in asserting that the experience of emptiness is due to the alienation of modern society. The psychodynamic school tends to lay the cause of the experience at the doorstep of early childhood experience, which is itself, of course, a function of social conditions.

The psychoanalytic explanations, unlike the other explanations for the experience, refer to developmental considerations in the individual's history and also refer to intrapsychic agencies and their interactions as contributing to the etiology of the experience of emptiness. The other schools of thought either de-emphasize or abjure this approach.

One overriding concern that pervades the whole of this discourse is the lack of the definition of the term or experience under discussion. While many of the descriptions of the experience are indeed eloquent and evocative, there is a great lack of precision in the definition of the concept.

Having examined some of the approaches to understanding this experience in various schools of thought, we now turn towards establishing the theoretical foundations of this effort.

Theory of Emotional Development or The Theory of Positive Disintegration

The theory of positive disintegration, or aspects of it, is delineated in a number of volumes: Dabrowski, Kawczak and Piechowski (1970), Dabrowski (1967). The fullest exposition of the theory, however, is to be found in Dabrowski and Piechowski (1977).

The theory of positive disintegration (TPD) states that there are five hierarchically organized levels of development. The process of development involves a transcending of an earlier structure through its disintegration and ultimate restructuring into a new structure. Thus, disintegration is seen as positive, as being a necessary process for development to occur.

The Levels of Development

<u>Level I- Primary Integration:</u>

At this level the person is organized around the meeting of basic survival needs. The person at this stage feels relatively well integrated, and has, as his primary purpose the meeting of "instinctual" needs, e.g., hunger, sex, safety, shelter, comfort. It seems as though the person is dealing primarily with what Maslow (1968) "basic needs" and not "meta-needs." The individual at this level of development is unaware of meta-needs, or if he is aware of them, assimilates them to his primary orientation of meeting basic needs. This would occur in much the same fashion that Kohlberg (1976) has demonstrated that people of lower levels of moral development interpret and assimilate the acts of higher moral development entirely in the terms of lower moral development, that is, they interpret altruistic acts as being acts of meeting basic needs.

Level II - Unilevel Disintegration:

At this level the relatively smooth functioning of level I breaks up, disintegrates and leaves the person with a predominantly wavering attitude. The previously well-bound and integrated structure now becomes loose, resulting in the individual feeling attacks of directionlessness and chaos. There is a difficulty in making decisions; forces within the person push against one another so that the person vacillates. In the absence of an internal hierarchical organization (the disintegration is unilevel) the forces do not resolve into smooth and deliberate action. The person at this stage is very subject to polarities of emotion. Sometimes the disintegration can be extreme and result in psychosis. In other instances, the person can "pull themselves together" and manage to function in a seemingly integrated way. Under pressure, however, the disintegration returns. Frequently people at this stage long for a return to the "good old days" of Primary Integration, when things seemed, by comparison, simple. The words of Yeats' poem (1989) seem to capture Unilevel Disintegration quite aptly:

Things fall apart, the center cannot hold,
Mere anarchy is loosed upon the world.

Level III - Spontaneous Multilevel Disintegration:

At this level of development, things are still fallen apart, but there is a growing hierarchization within the person. Instead of equipotent forces acting upon each other, resulting in a wavering, vacillating directionlessness, there is a developing sense of a hierarchy of values, with certain values and forces emerging as prepotent. The person begins to feel "inferiority towards himself," that is, he starts to experience the difference between what he is and what he ought to be. This develops out of the newly-emerging hierarchy of aims and values. Among some of the other "dynamisms" (or experiences that can facilitate and encourage further development) are: positive maladjustment, feelings of guilt, feelings of shame, astonishment with oneself, disquietude with oneself, inferiority towards oneself, hierarchization, subject-object in oneself, inner psychic transformation and self-awareness, self-control, autopsychotherapy and education-of-oneself.

Level IV - Organized Multilevel Disintegration

In this stage the person has developed an organized and consistent hierarch within him or herself. In the words of Ogburn (1976):

> He has transcended the problem of becoming
> And tackles the problems of being. (Ogburn, 1976)

The basics needs are generally well taken care of at this stage; the individual is concerned largely with the meta-needs that Maslow speaks of. Maslow (1968, p. 210). In fact, Piechowski (1978) argues that there is a strong correspondence between the Self Actualizing person of Maslow's thinking and the person who has achieved Level IV. Thus, some of the active dynamisms are: self-awareness, knowledge of one's uniqueness, developmental needs, existential responsibility, self-control, regulating one's own development, education-of-oneself, self-induced programs of systematic development. The primary task of the individual at this stage of development is to solidify the structure that emerges from the previous disintegrated stage.

The locus of control for the individual at Level IV is very firmly an internal one—one can act independently of the external environment if one so chooses.

Level V -Secondary Integration

Only a few rare individuals reach this level of development. At this stage, the "ought" has become unified with "what is." The personality ideal has been achieved. The planful self-development of Level IV has been successfully completed.

Overexcitabilities

Development through the stages is related, in large part to the level of excitability in the person. Dabrowski posits five types of overexcitabilities: Emotional, Psychomotor, Sensual, Intellectual and

Imaginational. An overexcitability is a predisposition in the individual, largely inherited, to respond to certain types of stimuli in an above average manner. For example, a person with sensual overexcitability will be more responsive than average to cutaneous stimulation. He or she will also tend, if this tends to be his or her dominant type of overexcitability, to transform other types of experience, e.g., emotional, intellectual, imaginational into sensual types of experience. For example, the emotion of affection will be readily transformed into stroking for a person with sensual overexcitability.

Perhaps another term for overexcitability would be sensitivity, perhaps like photographic paper which can be varied in its sensitivity to various types of light input. The overexcitability would correspond to a finely grained, highly sensitized paper—the impression of reality gained when there is an overexcitability is correspondingly sharp, intense and vivid.

Following is a brief overview of the manifestations of the various forms of overexcitabilities:

Sensual:

This manifests through a heightened sensitivity to sensual experience—skin stimulation, sexual excitability, the desire for stroking, physical comfort, etc.

Psychomotor:

This manifests itself in a tendency for vigorous movement, violent games and sports, rapid talk and a pressure to be moving. Emotional excitement is converted into movement that is highly charged with energy.

Imaginational:

This is shown in a sensitivity to the imagined possibilities of things. There is a rich association of images and metaphors flow freely.

Intellectual:

In his the individual displays a voracious curiosity and desire to learn and understand. There is a persistence in asking probing questions and a reverence for logic.

Emotional:

> This is the most important overexcitability in that if this is absent or weak, it is unlikely that development will proceed. Emotional overexcitability is manifested in the person's ability to form strong emotional attachments to others, and living things and places. Also present with emotional overexcitability are: concern about death, strong affective memory, concern for others, empathy, exclusive relationships and feelings of loneliness.

The level of development the individual reaches is dependent upon three factors: The first factor is the person's hereditary endowment, namely, the configuration of his overexcitabilities. The second factor is the environment in which the individual lives and the extent to which it supports or impedes that individual's development. The third factor consists of the individual's response to his situation—the decisions he makes in responses to the life situation he finds himself in and the genetic heritage that he possesses.

Given this framework, one may take the next conjectural step and hypothesize the intensity, frequency and form of experiences of emptiness for each of the various levels of emotional development.

The Hypothesized Experience of Emptiness at Different Levels of Emotional Development

Level I

At level one the experience of emptiness is extremely rare. There is little introspection or empathy at this level, and the experience of emptiness, if experienced at all, will be very swiftly squashed or eradicated through vigorous movement, loud noise or some other unreflective activity.

Since there is little concern over death at his level, except in very rudimentary ways, it is almost impossible for existential emptiness to be experienced, that is, an empty feeling associated with concerns about the meaning of life, with one's authenticity or purpose or with the nature of one's true self.

The conformism of this level of development also contributes to the inability to experience existential vacuum. The experience of existential vacuum rests upon a questioning of the "given" order of things. This questioning is impossible without the person being open, to some degree, to non-conformity.

Level II

The wavering ambitendency characteristic of level two functioning can frequently give a "no-exit" quality to the individual's thought processes and feelings. From such a battle of equipotential forces can emerge a sense of futility. The no-exit quality of the individual's life can lead to a seemingly purposeless round-robin of conflicting ideas and feelings, leading to a sense of paralysis and meaninglessness accompanied by feelings of emptiness resulting from the sense of not having a coherent, consistent self. This is phase of "many selves." These conflicting selves, all operating on a unilevel basis, vie with one another creating an inner sense of chaotic disintegration.

The sense of existential vacuum can also occur if a person is precipitated rapidly from level one functioning to level two functioning. In this instance, novel information, or a disruptive emotional experience or a rapid environmental change might overthrow the previously existing sense of integration. This is truly when "things fall apart" and "the center cannot hold." It is a though, in information processing parlance, there is an overload of positive feedback exceeding the system's current ability to recode, resulting in inner disruption and confusion. Frequently, this disruption involves an assault on cherished attitudes about self and the world. The breaking down of these attitudes can result in the individual feeling a deep sense of meaninglessness and an emptiness arising out of an uncertainty as to his identity.

There also is likely a yearning for "the good old days" of Primary Integration. Suicide is possible at these points.

The following excerpt from an interview with subject "G" in the initial stages of my research gives a picture of this sort of situation and an individual's experience of it. "G" was brought up in a rather strict religious family, and the move from home to college precipitated many values conflicts and deep-rooted changes that resulted in an internal sense of numbness or emptiness.

> G: So there was this juxtaposition of these: best friend sexually involved, parents against boyfriend, boyfriend loves and accepts me the way parents don't. I want sexual involvement to some extent with boyfriend but the church says its wrong, I love God, erm, and so this one day I was really falling apart, I was just in tears...and I was praying in the chapel and I came back to my room and my roommate who had been encouraging my friend to have the sexual exploits came in and informed me that she was moving out of the room, and leaving me with her (laughter)...after that for the next week or so I walked around in a real daze, it was like a values crisis of the first order. And I really had to sort out my priorities and loyalties and it was very hard.

Interviewer: So when your network of friends changed, it brought on an ethical crisis and that brought on a feeling of emptiness?

G: Yeah. There was for one thing a total loss of order in the world...yeah...

Interviewer: Things were falling apart?

G: Yeah right. It was very hard to understand what you could hold on to and feel good about, you know?

Level III

At level three, the existential vacuum is a hierarchical phenomenon. Existential vacuum is experienced much more empathically, that is, the experiences of others or one's observations of the world can trigger existential vacuum.

The search to know oneself has truly begun at this level. This search, in itself, is strewn with pitfalls of experiencing existential vacuum. At this level, the experience of existential vacuum is highly reflective and often has to do with the unmet desire for authenticity and knowledge of oneself.

At this level, the concept of existential courage, as described by Tillich (1952) comes into play since it is a very important determinant of the reaction to existential emptiness. Frankl's concept of existential vacuum, in some of its forms would fit into this level of development also, although much of what he talks about seems to be more clearly a level two type of emptiness, not especially tied to existential concerns, but mainly growing out of an inner vacuousness. Existential courage can help in directing the individual to higher levels of development.

As intimated in the work of Sartre (1957) who claims that a "Personal project," with its concomitant awareness of the tension between "what is" and "what ought to be" creates the experience of emptiness we would again predict existential emptiness to be frequently experienced at this level of development when this concern takes on a powerful and existential meaning (Dabrowski and Piechowski, 1977).

At level two "what is and what ought to be" are conceived in terms that are not existential. The emptiness that thus ensues from the project is thus not existential in nature, that is, it is a plain unadorned emptiness, perhaps the most painful and hopeless-feeling sort of all.

Level IV

At this level the experience of existential vacuum may be very rare indeed since the individual has solved many of the problems that beset the person at level three. The psychological structures are far more organized than at lower levels so the experience of inner lack is likely to be infrequent. The individual does strive for self-perfection in aiming towards the "personality ideal" (Dabrowski and Piechowski, 1977) and this might predispose the individual to the experience of emptiness were it not for the fact by the time the person has reached level four he or she is in touch with their feeling life and has developed what

Rogers (1961) calls the capacity to "be in process." That is, the individual can lay claim, at this level to the capacity for what Dewey (1938) calls "means/ends fusion," thus reducing the experience of the gap between what is and what ought to be.

Infrequent spasms of existential emptiness or emptiness may be experienced under stress of fatigue or illness, but these should be passing since the person has at this level a highly integrated sense of purpose and meaning. Existential concern remains high however. As Maddi (1967) and Rogers (1961) assert, "doubt is an essential part of the ideal personality." Maslow, too, (1968) stresses that self-actualizing people can live with uncertainty.

Level V

Existential vacuum at this level is virtually impossible or, as seems to be the case with certain individuals like Gautama Buddha or Saint Francis of Assisi, it becomes integrated into a living experience of religious belief.

The Experience Of Emptiness: An Integration

The findings of Hazell (1984a, 1984b, 1989) bear significant relation to the broad array of literature reported in chapter two of this study. It is the purpose of this section to discuss the nature and import of some of the discrepancies between the findings of the above-mentioned research and those found in the literature. Four major points emerge. They are:

a. The psychological literature does not differentiate adequately between the experiences of emptiness and existential emptiness.

b. The psychological literature does not adequately distinguish between the experience of emptiness and its assumed objective presence, and this creates significant errors.

c. The psychological literature is incorrect in arguing that the experience of emptiness is pathological, for it is directly related to emotional development.

d. The literature often does not adequately account for the importance of personality features such as values-structure or over-excitability profile in mediating the level of the experience of emptiness.

In some examples of the literature, all four of the above criticisms apply, in others, only one or two apply. By and large, however, the bodies of literature and work that garner most consistent support from the results of this research are the artistic works, Eastern religions, existential philosophy, namely, the works of Camus, Kierkegaard and Sartre, and those writers in the other fields who seem to have integrated these thinkers into their efforts. More detailed divagations on these themes constitute the remainder of this subsection.

Kierkegaard, for example (1846) argues that the "revelation of emptiness" signifies a move from "immediacy" or absence of self-reflection to a state of self-reflection. This shift, which is essentially developmental in nature, entails the initiation of a dialectical process within the personality of the individual, an initiation of objectification of the self. The parallels between this shift in awareness and the developmental shift in the theory of emotional development from level one (primary integration) to level two (unilevel disintegration) and further into level three (multilevel disintegration) are quite numerous and telling. The revelation of emptiness occurs then, as part of the developmental process. The psychopathic individual, who can be regarded as an "ideal type" example of lack of emotional development (see Cleckley, 1976) would, by extrapolation of the findings in this research score very low on the experienced level of emptiness scale. In these individuals the experience of emptiness is only revealed subjectively as the individual moves into levels two and three of emotional development.

This line of thought is extremely close to the thought of Sartre, as reported in chapter two. Sartre, it will be remembered, asserts that the experience of emptiness emerges when the individual gains consciousness. Emptiness arises, he argues, when the individual reflects upon himself and the consequent "gap" or "vacancy" between observer and observed is experienced as an internal void or emptiness. This internal emptiness is also experienced when the person takes on their self as a "project." The distance between what is at present and what will be in the future of the self is experienced again as emptiness. For Sartre, the subjective experience of emptiness is the price humans pay in the movement from being "massif," mindless and unreflective, "like inkwells," to becoming self-aware human individuals, who must then struggle relentlessly, like Prometheus or Sisyphus, with the burden of consciousness, either suffering because of the knowledge gathered from higher levels or engaged in an unremitting upward striving.

The experience of emptiness, thus, is the price of freedom, and again, the parallels between Sartre's scheme of thought and the developmental stages of the theory of emotional development are clear. Level one corresponds to the lack of self-awareness that Sartre talks about. At this level we find individuals who are "massif" or who are attempting, through acts of "mauvaise foi" or "being for others," to retain primary integration. To these individuals, the subjective experience of emptiness is not revealed. It has been shown how the revelation of emptiness is dependent upon level of emotional development and that this development, in turn, is dependent upon the profile of overexcitabilities of the person.

With the beginnings of self-reflection in level two of emotional development and its furtherance and increased existential coloring at higher levels of development, the experience of emptiness emerges into consciousness.

Therefore, the findings of this research are consonant with the theories of Kierkegaard, Sartre and existential philosophy in general. The logic of this support runs as follows: The experience of emptiness is a direct function of emotional development. Emotional development, as measured in this research, implies an increase in self-reflection. The existential philosophers, Sartre and Kierkegaard argue that the experience of emptiness emerges into awareness with the onset of self-reflection. The arguments of Sartre and Kierkegaard therefore find support here.

In addition, it is interesting to note that Dabrowski's theory is probably influenced very strongly by the thought of Kierkegaard since Dabrowski himself found great meaning in the writings of Kierkegaard. The fact that Kierkegaard posited a developmental theory with levels that correspond in form to the theory of emotional development, namely, a progression from the "aesthetic" to the "ethical" and the "religious," provides a capstone to the argument that this research provides empirical support for aspects of existential philosophy, notably the thought of Sartre and Kierkegaard.

Thus, this research tends to support the notion that emptiness revealed is perhaps cause for celebration, albeit a bittersweet one, for it seems to betoken an internal shift in the self-awareness of the individual. One can imagine it metaphorically as the experience the jammed polar ice pack could have of itself in spring, when its massive, locked and compressed contents start to melt and break up, expanding and changing form. The spaces between the ice floes would be experienced by the ice sheet as emptiness. In the human being, the break-up from primary integration is like the breaking up of packed soil by a farmer's harrow, which gives good tilth, an optimal crumb-structure and enables growth to take place.

Emptiness concealed occurs at the stage of primary integration. Metaphorically the ice never melts and the soil remains compact, airless and infertile.

It is this distinction, namely that between emptiness concealed and emptiness revealed, that has escaped many of the psychological writers cited in this chapter. Sartre and Kierkegaard make this distinction. The clinical writers, however, treat the subjective experience of emptiness and the objective presence of emptiness in the same way, failing to distinguish between the two with adequate clarity. The emptiness in this research is emptiness revealed, i.e. it measures the subjective experience of emptiness. This would mean that a person could lead what might be judged by others to be a very empty life, but be unaware of it and would consequently score low on the E or EX scale (measures of emptiness (E) and existential emptiness (Ex), Hazell, 1984b). This research shows that this person would in all likelihood be at a lower level of emotional development and would have a specific profile with regard to overexcitabilities and values.

The failure in the literature to distinguish between emptiness that is in the subjective awareness of the individual and emptiness that is not in the subjective awareness of the individual and emptiness that is not in the awareness of the individual has led, given the results of this research, to some important erroneous omissions and commissions. Outside of existential philosophy, Eastern religions and the arts, there is little indication that the experience of emptiness is directly related to emotional or any kind of personal development. Rather, the experience of emptiness is seen as pathological. In most psychoanalytical writings it is seen as resulting from distorted object relations, faulty and inappropriate empathic responses, developmental arrests, regression and so on.

Miller (1981) and Bruch (1973) relate the experience of emptiness to developmental potential and the inherited personality profile of the individual.

Miller argues that the experience of emptiness is especially likely in gifted individuals who are prone to being "used" by their parents by virtue of their increased sensitivity and responsiveness to the needs of others. Two of the three components in Miller's explanation of the experience of emptiness find support in this research. First, there are indications in this research that individuals with intellectual overexcitability are prone to the experience of emptiness. It has been shown (Piechowski et al., 1982) that gifted individuals have high levels of intellectual and emotional overexcitability. Therefore the notion that Miller proposes that there is a relationship between giftedness and the experience of emptiness finds support here in that the experience of emptiness has been found to be directly related to intellectual overexcitability.

Secondly, the hypothesis Miller forwards that individuals who are more sensitive to the needs of others also finds support here, in that concern and empathy for others increases with level of emotional development, and this research shows a direct correlation with experienced level of emptiness and level of emotional development. As to the third component in her model of the etiology of emptiness, namely the usage of the child by the parents, we have no available evidence to support or reject it.

Once again, we arrive at the conclusion that the subjective experience of emptiness seems related, not to pathology or ill health, but to the process of emotional development.

Bruch (1979) reports that patients diagnosed with anorexia nervosa and who report heightened levels of the experience of emptiness are very frequently academically gifted individuals. This finding is consonant with the findings of this research (Hazell 1984a), in that there appears here to be a correlation between intellectual overexcitability, theoretical interest and experienced level of emptiness. What Bruch does not mention or sufficiently stress in her theoretical statements is that the struggle that the anorexics are involved in is potentially a developmental struggle that emerges not so much from deficits as from a certain profile of overexcitabilities in the individual and a heightened developmental potential. Bruch and many other writers in the field of psychology could be criticized for being too quick to impugn the efforts of the parents of their patients when so little is known, relatively speaking, in the field of psychology itself about the psychological processes involved in higher levels of emotional development. For example, the so-called pathological experience of emptiness in the clinical literature is often related to parental failure. Masterson (1972, p. 61) states that the experience of void, springs partially from introjection of mother's "negative attitudes." Given that this research has demonstrated that the experience of emptiness is related to level of emotional development and a specific profile of overexcitabilities, this approach that is frequently found is in need of modification. The modification called for is not to diminish the recognized importance of "positive attitudes" but to increase the appreciation in counselors and parents alike of the special vulnerabilities and consequent challenges and requirements that exist in individuals with certain overexcitability profiles, values orientations and developmental potential.

While we cannot be sure that the experiences of emptiness that Bruch reports in her anorexic patients are the same as the phenomenon being measured in this research, we do have some ground for asking whether or not the intense experiences of emptiness are here also signs of potential emotional development.

Many of the other writers cited in chapter two, miss this point, because they miss the difference between emptiness revealed and emptiness concealed. In their haste to attack and denigrate emptiness concealed, they overlook and crush the developmental potential of which emptiness revealed is the signature.

Thus for Kohut, Kernberg and Masterson, for example, the experience of emptiness is seen as entirely pathological. It is not viewed as a "potential space" from which the individual may advance or retreat. While the treatments may be appropriate, modifications in their conceptualizations of the experience would seem to be called for in the light of the results presented here. First, none of these writers recognize the contribution of overexcitabilities and values orientation to the experience of emptiness. This research shows them to be significant contributors to the level of this experience in the individual. Secondly, none of these writers make distinctions between emptiness and existential emptiness. This research has shown that these two forms of emptiness behave in very different manners and are related to very different personality variables such as level of emotional development and profile of overexcitabilities. Thirdly, none of these writers make the necessary distinctions between the subjective experience of emptiness and the objective presence of emptiness. Because of this they do not see that emptiness, subjectively experienced, is directly related to the process of emotional development. They do seem aware of the processes of "mauvaise foi" that can be used by the individual as a means of avoiding the experience of emptiness, and here they are somewhat in accord with the existential philosophers. However, they fail, again and again, to see the developmental import of the experience of emptiness.

Thus, when the person "develops a psychic surface that is out of contact with an active nuclear self" (Kohut, 1977, p. 59), it is rightly regarded as a painful state of affairs. What Kohut, in this instance, fails to point out is that when the individual experiences a glimmering awareness of this alienation and ensuing feeling of emptiness, and embarks on the dialectic struggle between "real self" and "false self," it constitutes an initiation of the processes of multilevel emotional development. It is as if Kohut and the other psychoanalytic writers believe that emotional development can proceed without awareness of non-being and the concomitant "revelation of emptiness." These beliefs do not find support in this research.

The capacity to experience emptiness may be viewed in a theoretically similar manner as the capacity for depression, guilt and concern for others inasmuch as these are relatively absent a the lower levels of development but increase and become more finely modulated by empathy and self-awareness as the developmental process proceeds. Ogburn (1976) has demonstrated how theoretically the form of the experience of guilt changes with the level of emotional development. Some beginning support has been given in this research to the notion that the experience of emptiness undergoes similar transformations according to level of development.

There are grounds, therefore, for calling into question the rampant pathologizing of the experience of emptiness that occurs not only in most of the psychoanalytic literature, but also in the literature of the so-called "existential psychologists." What is severely lacking in each of these bodies of thought is the recognition that, while the individual experiencing emptiness may well have suffered from early developmental deficits, the very experience of emptiness, in awareness, is a sign that the person has emerged from being "massif" (level one) and has thus joined the struggle, each in his or her own unique way, towards emotional development. Emptiness viewed in this light may be truly cause for celebration, for it is close to being a psychological rebirth, the birth of the potential of the person to possess and become a true self rather than an unreflective, externally adapted, "massif" false self system. Laing (1969) is one of the rare psychoanalytic writers who is aware of the developmental potential augured by the sense of inner poverty and emptiness associated with the self that is thus divided. Sartre theorizes that it is the division of the self into observer and observed that creates the feeling of emptiness. This division of the self into knower and known creates knowledge of the self or the potential for knowledge of the self. Once the fruit of the tree of knowledge is eaten, the banishment from the "Eden" of primary integration is complete, one is consigned to human existence and would be able to return were it possible, to primary integration only through self-destruction or self-deceit.

On one thing all the writers cited in this research seem to agree: all are fully aware of the "regressive pull" of primary integration, although all use different terminology to describe the processes involved. The findings of this research seem to indicate, however, that much of what psychologically-oriented writers and others regard as "flight from freedom" or as "defensive acting-out" may be related to inherent psychological features of the individual, such as a high degree of economic interest or sensual overexcitability and a low degree of intellectual overexcitability, or theoretical interest.

Neither Frankl nor May admit of different personality features that might predispose the individual towards or away from the experience of emptiness. That such features or traits exert an influence has been shown in Hazell (1984a). Neither writers adequately distinguish the difference between emptiness and existential emptiness and this confusion is more prevalent in the work of Frankl (see pages 26-27). What is lacking in the thought of these writers is the concept of level of development and the impact this has on both the experienced level of emptiness and the meaning of the term itself. Neither admits of the possibility of the experience of emptiness being related to level of development or distinct personality features. They also fail to distinguish between the subjective experience of emptiness and its objective presence, and this leads them astray, for they commit the same error as the psychoanalytic writers in that they pathologize an experience which this research shows to be directly correlated with emotional development. Frankl, for example, regards the experience of emptiness as a failure—a failure of responsibility, faith and of appreciating the whole being. While this may be true of the person who is empty but does not feel empty, we now know this assertion to be false in regard to the person who feels empty, for increases in emotional development imply at least a modicum of an increase in responsibility, faith and appreciating the whole being. In fact, the individual at level five is a veritable avatar of these qualities. The subjective experience of emptiness, in the light of the results of this research, represents an emergence of responsibility, faith and appreciating the whole being, and conversely the individual who does not experience emptiness is, in all likelihood, according to the results of this research, severely lacking in capacity for responsibility, faith and appreciating the whole being.

It could be argued, though not terribly plausibly, that Frankl is discussing the developmental shift from level three of emotional development to level four when a decrease in the experienced level of emptiness is hypothesized to occur. If this is the case, further serious modifications would need to be made to his theory in the light of research on the theory of emotional development. He would need, for example, to relate this theory to the overexcitability profile of the individual and also to the fact that the number of persons achieving level four of emotional development is presently rather small.

May commits the same error as all the other psychological writers (save Laing, Miller and Winnicott) in that he does not differentiate emptiness revealed from emptiness concealed and ends up pathologizing a growth process. May attacks the experience of emptiness when this is not the danger. The danger comes from the emptiness that is objectively present but not experienced.

Kurt Vonnegut (1976) compares artists to canaries in the mine. In the old days, miners took canaries down the mine so that when there was poison gas, the canaries would die. This would warn the more robust miners that there was poison around and that they should leave before they died either from asphyxiation or from an explosion. The artists cited at the outset of this research were, of course, performing a similar function in that they were revealing emptiness, helping it enter the field of awareness, facilitating its shift from an objective, but remarked upon presence to a subjective and widely-discussed experience.

Charles Darwin tells us that it is precisely the function of art to "sap the moralistic timidity" that prevents us from examining feeling states and attitudes that were previously regarded as off-bounds. Thus the artists mentioned in chapters one and two of this study can be seen as venturing into psychological experiences at the very border of human comprehension, and attempting, through artistic expression, to bring order to them, to communicate them, and perhaps to hear some response to their message. The explorations of these artists were often intensely personal, and this is also true of the philosophers, notably Kierkegaard. The artistic and philosophical self-discipline, however, rendered these efforts and explorations available to further study and experience.

Baker (1969), writes the following of Hemingway:

> A *Clean, Well-Lighted Place* was autobiographical only in the sense that it offered a brief look into the underside of Ernest's spiritual world, the nightmare of nothingness by which he was still haunted.
>
> (Baker, 1969)

The struggle to grasp and comprehend the feeling, is, for Hemingway, a personal one. The reader is led, in reading the few pages of this short story, to examine, perhaps perplexedly, the underside of his own world, perhaps with a sudden revelation of his own emptiness. Or perhaps this journey to the underside of one's spiritual world is familiar to the reader and the story serves more as comforting evidence that one is not alone, that others too are haunted by these experiences. Given that elsewhere in his writings, Hemingway examines the theme of responsibility, as he does in *For Whom the Bell Tolls*, we may venture the hypothesis that he was involved in the process of multilevel emotional development.

Both Tolstoy and Dostoievsky treat the experience of emptiness as it arises in the face of death, in front of the firing squad, or on the battlefield. Both relate these experiences to emotional development. For Dostoievsky, there was an enlightenment experience whilst waiting to go before the firing squad. Pierre, in *War and Peace* undergoes a similar self-transforming experience in the face of his own moment of execution. Prior to this, Prince Andrei, on the battlefield at Austerlitz, experiences his own nothingness as he is wounded and falls from his horse.

In *Darkness at Noon,* Koestler describes the condemned man having "oceanic experiences" of "self-dissolution" as the intense self-transformation potentiated by impending death takes place. In the final scene, when he is shot, he experiences himself as a "shrug of eternity." The descriptions of all of these writers find support in this research. The confronting of one's death in the form of increased existential concern is related to the experience of emptiness and creates the experience of existential emptiness, and this, in turn, has been found to be highly related to the process of self-transformation as described in the theory of emotional development. These writers, each in a dramatic way, present the reality of death and the self-transformation that accrues with the confrontation of that reality. As the Zen saying goes, "He who thinks upon his own death will surely attain enlightenment." (Suzuki, 1956)

Beckett and Kafka seem to not only confront the experience of emptiness but to take us right into it, and live it. In the works of these artists, we see a world where all meaning has been steamrollered flat. These are living examples of the "type C communicative field" that Langs (1979) describes. To read these novels or view these plays or to examine the paintings of Hopper and Tooker is to see emptiness revealed, an emptiness that lurks beneath our everyday awareness. These artists have not shrunk in moralistic timidity from the experience of emptiness, but they have responded to it creatively. In this response, and in the sharing of this response in living forms, they help others confront and respond to the experience themselves. In Beckett, for example, there is much wry and ironic humor, that helps us cope with the experience. Kafka leaves the experience stark and still imbued with its original terror, serving as a testament of the extreme sensitivity of the man himself.

Each of these artists shows us that a response to the experience of emptiness is possible, that it may be transcended. And the writer Tillich provides an understanding of how it may be transcended. The experience of emptiness arises, says Tillich, owing to a crushing of the creative life of man—a negation of his spiritual being. The above writers show us that even when the emptiness is absolute, that it may be responded to creatively. This creative response to the experience of void is what Tillich calls the "Courage to Be" or the "Courage to be as Part." This courage emanates from what Kierkegaard calls the "will" which sustains the eternal dialectic within the self or from what is called the "disposing and directing center" in the theory of emotional development. In the theory of emotional development, the disposing and directing center emerges in fuller force as the individual moves from level three development to levels four and five. What is being argued here is that one of the major functions of the disposing and directing center is the creation of meaning through courageous and creative response in the face of its negation and annulment. It has been shown here that the experience of emptiness is directly related to emotional development. If this is the case, then the manner in which the individual responds to the experience of emptiness is of importance in that these responses lay the groundwork for future development. The artists so far mentioned and many of the Christian existentialists, for example, Tillich, provide guidelines to the individual in responding to the experience of emptiness.

It is the nature of one's response to emptiness that Camus is speaking of when he transcends, in *The Rebel*, the apparent contradiction between the logical inconsistency of the nihilistic position on the one hand and the objective "absurdity" of human life on the other hand. This transcendence is accomplished through an act of existential courage, through an act of will. One stands in relation to the negation of the universe not as "un revolutionnaire," but as "un homme revolté" who accepts the burden of the absurdity of this stance. This is what Sartre (1964) is speaking of when he talks of "the nothingness that is made to be in the heart of man."

These artists and philosophers, therefore, give us a "map" as it were, for dealing with these experiences of emptiness. They are social and individual therapists who serve as beacons to those embarked on the process of emotional growth. They are only a beacon, for the actual work of development is always the responsibility of the individual.

The response to the experience of emptiness is fraught with dangers, and again the artists, philosophers and theologians provide assistance in charting these sometimes dangerous waters. Dostoievsky, in *Crime and Punishment* demonstrates, with all the rigor of a formal theory, that the total freedom that is a logical consequence of inner emptiness, is illusory, for in the final analysis Raskolnikov feels guilt and, in the final paragraphs, hope. Again, the nihilistic position is demonstrated to be untenable. As Thomas Mann states in *Mario and the Magician*, "a will that is directed towards its own freedom thrusts into emptiness." These writers, therefore, seem agreed that the experience of emptiness requires a creative response. None underestimate the difficulty of his task. All recognize that it is related to personal development and growth. The experiences of emptiness described in the lives of Jesus Christ and Saint Francis of Assisi serve as examples for how extreme the experience of emptiness can be and how terrible, impossible and yet ineluctable is the demand for creative response.

This research provides much support for many of the ideas forwarded by the artists and theological writers so far mentioned. These writers, however, go one step further than this research in that they make explicit recommendations in terms of what are the most profitable ways of responding to the experience of emptiness when one has it. This topic of the response to emptiness is not dealt with in most of the psychoanalytic writings since they regard the experience as pathological and as something to be "cured" rather than responded to. This is not true of Winnicott who provides extremely fertile ideas in this area, and it is not true of R.D. Laing who is, especially in this, an existentially-influenced psychoanalytic writer.

To a greater or lesser extent, the existential psychologists deal with the issue of the response to the experience of emptiness in ways that are clearly derived from their artistic, philosophical and theological predecessors. May, for example, posits the concept of existential courage which is the same as the "Courage to Be" of his teacher, Tillich, who in turn owes this concept of Kierkegaard. Frankl speaks of "responsibility" in reaction to the existential vacuum and this is a derivative of Tillich's notion of "moral self-affirmation."

Maddi (1967) does not provide notions as to the response to the experience of emptiness, but he does provide a formal and substantive model which has to do with the etiology of the existential neurosis, and thus, by association, of the etiology of the experience of emptiness which is a symptom of this. The results of this stud, then to support certain aspects of his formal model, but refute and reject all of the aspects of his substantive model.

Formally, Maddi asserts that the existential neurosis is created by a combination of certain personality features and environmental stressor which acts in the way of a "releaser" of the neurosis. This research addressed the aspect of the model that had to do with the personality features that predispose the individual to the experience of emptiness, a symptom of the existential neurosis. The exploration of the "releasers" of this experience awaits further study. In that the experience of emptiness was indeed predicted by certain personality features, the formal model presented by Maddi holds.

However, Maddi asserts that the personality that is predisposed towards existential neurosis (and by extension emptiness) is "overly concrete and fragmentary," "too much concerned with living a successful life" and "nonhumanistic." The findings of this research reveal exactly the opposite. The experienced level of emptiness and existential emptiness increase with increasing abstractness, decrease with increasing concreteness and economic concern, decrease with increasing sensualism and increase with increasing level of emotional development which imply increases in humanism, abstractness, cognitive complexity and a questioning of conformity.

The group that Maddi identifies as being "premorbid" with regard to the existential neurosis is incorrect in the light of this research which shows that the experienced level of emptiness and existential emptiness rest upon higher levels of intellectual overexcitability and developmental level among other personality features.

Maddi commits his error in that he fails to distinguish between the experience of emptiness and its objective but unexperienced presence. If we were to adopt Maddi's definition of the premorbid character we would include many individuals who, in the light of this research, by virtue of their limited developmental potential, their undistinguished overexcitability profile and their values orientation, would never experience emptiness except in its most muted and evanescent forms. The precipitating stresses that Maddi includes in his model will only, it would seem, induce an existential neurosis in the individual if there is the responsive pre-existing personality structure. Maddi's use of the term "premorbid" is also questionable in the light of the fact that the experience of emptiness is related in this research to emotional development. "Premorbidity" is hardly an appropriate term for a state of growth-readiness.

Winnicott (1971) provides an extremely fertile and useful concept that bridges and fits much of what has been discussed thus far. It is the concept of potential space. The experience of emptiness may be regarded as the creation within the self of a "space," analogous, in many ways to the gaps of which Sartre writes. Metaphorically, this space may be regarded as a stage before the scenery has been put up and before the actors enter.

The image is fitting for it is in this potential space, which is first embodies in the space that emerges and grows between the mother and the infant, that play, and ultimately self-realization can occur. When something is amiss, the potential space is obliterated, that is, is boundaries contract or expand to create a space that is infinitesimally small or infinitely large, and thus, unavailable for creative response. There is no tension, there is no anxiety but there is no play and thus the formation of symbols and the developmental processes are held up.

The developmental processes with regard to his potential space may be viewed as follows. As the infant starts to differentiate self from other (Mahler, 1975; Hoffer, 1951) he or she is presented with a potential "space." Under optimal conditions, the infant may respond to this empty space, which may consist of simply "being in the presence of the mother," in a fashion that is essentially a creative response. The creative response takes the form of play. The creative response is itself dependent initially on the provision of an adequate "holding environment" that both allows the formation of the potential space that, on the one hand, does not engulf, flood and thereby obliterate the potential space and on the other hand, provides secure boundaries to the space so that the meaning of the creative response is contained and is not allowed to dissipate into an unbounded void.

The former, overconstricted holding environment, is parallel to Kierkegaard's notion of the "despair of finitude." The latter, unbounded space, leads to the despair of infinitude. In both instances the creative response is either rendered impossible or annulled. Durkheim (1951) in analyzing the social fabrics that lead to increased incidences of suicide, demonstrates that the society that is over-individualistic and the society that is overly-stifling have increased suicide rates. This may be regarded as behavioral reactions on the social level to an inadequate holding environment and a consequent negation of the potential space. This research has shown, however, that developmental level and personality features also potentially play a role in this process.

It might be further theorized that under optimal conditions, the process of the creation of the potential space and the creative response to it are internalized, in a way that is parallel to the internalization of other psychic functions, for example, guilt or concern for others. The child will gradually develop in such a way that he creates his own "potential spaces" to which he must respond, in much the same way as children increase their asking of questions, or gradually increase the optimal distance between themselves and their mother-figure. In individuals with heightened overexcitabilities, for example, intellectual overexcitability, this process may be accelerated and will continue throughout their lives, giving rise to increased levels of the experience of emptiness.

The potential space is connected with self-realization and level of emotional development in that the creative response to the potential space, to the experience of emptiness, involves the use of symbols. At first, in the smallest of potential spaces, the symbol-play involves exploration of, and play with, the mother's face (Mahler, 1975). Later the space expands so that it may be manifested by, say, a sheet of blank paper between mother and child that the child draws upon and mother reacts to. The paper symbolizes the potential space, the emotional presence of the mother represents the holding environment and constitutes the boundaries to the space and the drawing of the infant constitutes the response to the potential space. The processes of symbol-formation and symbol-manipulation are now well on their way, as is the process of self-realization which rests on the creative use of symbols tied to a sense of personal meaning.

From these seeds grow the complex artistic endeavors, and theoretical efforts aimed at self-understanding. Before the artistic creation, and before the theoretical excursion, there needs must be the experience of emptiness, and while this experience may be occasioned by environmental deficits, there is evidence here to suggest that much of the experience of emptiness is due to the fact that it is an integral phase of the developmental process and is found in higher levels in persons of higher cognitive complexity and higher levels of intellectual overexcitability and theoretical interest.

The experiences around the potential space are thus deeply intertwined with emotional development. The space itself is like the empty page that confronts the poet or the writer or the blank canvas that the artist faces, or it is like the frame of the psychotherapeutic relationship. Personal freedom and development rest upon the creation of the initial void, for without this, the authentic creative response is annulled. These experiences are denied the individual who does not know and stand in relation to the empty spaces in the stream of life.

The body is the Bodhi tree,

The soul is like the mirror bright,

Take heed to keep it always clean,

And let not dust collect on it.

                    Shen-hsiu

The Bodhi is not like the tree

The mirror bright is nowhere shining,

As there is nothing from the first,

Where can the dust itself collect?

                    Hui-neng

Chapter 2

EMPTINESS AND RESISTANCE

Having posited the idea that the experience of emptiness is part and parcel of emotional growth "in statu nascendi," this portion aims at describing how the shying away from the often-disturbing aspects of the experience of emptiness serves to undermine emotional growth in the form of a resistance. The paper documents several of the ways in which this resistance shows itself and offers some ideas on how the therapist may be of assistance, or at least, not participate in anti-therapeutic activity.

I am aware that what I am about to write is enormously complex for me. In the face of this type of complexity, I find it best to start off with, and to return to, the personal, my heart and my relationships. These simplify.

I remember when I announced that my topic of research was to be the experience of emptiness, how I was the butt of many jokes and teasing. My supervisor, however, did not respond that way, when I mentioned my interests in our supervision group. He responded, "Emptiness is always good." I felt heartened and encouraged, and as was usual, prodded into further thought by his laconic remarks. I recalled how we spent such long spans of times in his sessions anxiously silent. The silence had many forms, many meanings. Much of the time, it was an empty silence. We were at an edge—a growth edge. We did not know what to do; yet we knew what had to be done. Perhaps someone had spoken of a certain type of fear or excitement or fantasy, and the supervisor had wondered if anyone else in the group felt that way. He asked, and then stepped back, leaving an empty space into which we could step, into which we could create something new. Certainly fear was a part of this experience; confusion too—perhaps even some resentment that he was not offering us enough help, support and guidance. While these emotions were essential, and often times were brought up as topics before the question at hand was dealt with, the key, for me, was the emptiness—the gap that was left for us to create into.   If one lost sight of this, forward progression would be stalled.

This scenario is probably familiar to any therapist or counselor. An interpretation is offered, an idea shared, a curiosity brought forward and—an empty space—sometimes minutes of silence in a group, sometimes a microsecond of faltering in an individual client—a moment or several moments, of blankness—as if one is facing a blank sheet of paper, or canvas or an empty stage—there is the challenge of the void.

This is the equivalent of Winnicott's (1965a) "moment of hesitation." Winnicott developed this concept while observing an asthmatic infant presented with an interesting looking shiny spatula. The infant wanted to reach the spatula, but before he could act on his desire, there was a "moment of hesitation." It was as if a terrific amount of psychosomatic self-organization had to go on before the impulse could be acted upon, before the empty space between the infant and the object of desire could be acknowledged and bridged and action created into this space—action emanating from the infant's own initiative—action the infant could claim as his very own. This required a number of factors—first, physical holding that contained but did not restrict movement or breathing; second, some reassurance that the good enough object would remain after the curious excursion; third, the capacity to organize oneself physiologically around the heightened state of excitement involved in the exploration. These being present, the infant could tolerate and bear the experience of emptiness inherent in this encounter with the new, learn and expand his range of possibilities.

The whole process would be short-circuited, and growth forestalled if Winnicott, or the mother had not provisioned the environment with the above three factors or if they had destroyed the intervening space by handing the infant the spatula. If they had not been capable of enduring the moment of hesitation themselves, but had had to fill it and bridge it or divert the infant's attention then a growth opportunity would have been collapsed. Typically, Winnicott does not say explicitly that this very dynamic had been present in the mother infant interaction and had contributed to the psychosomatic derailment of asthma, but, the implication seems to be there.

Back to groups. In the supervision group I mentioned at the outset and in many subsequent groups I have noticed this phenomenon of blankness that is in many ways isomorphic to Winnicott's "moment of hesitation." In a group that has been characterized by the common pattern of individuals sharing some sensitive information about themselves only to have it be routinely ignored by the rest of the group a discussion of the movie *Castaway* is initiated and continues for a few minutes. The group consultant remarks that this is what it feels like to be in this group—a castaway—isolated, unknown—cast-off. Following this comment there is—silence. A long silence, during which there is some fidgeting, surreptitious glancing at others, gazing out the room. The emotions seem to be complex—fear of saying something, anger at the consultant, guilt, some giggly excitement, a wish to leave and escape and a growing awareness of the empty space in the group's life. This is the moment of hesitation. Who will make the next move? At times it is like a standoff, as if the emptiness can be filled with a daredevil game of "chicken" or "who blinked first." At times it feels unbearable—so voided of meaning and flat, or so anguished in its shame that the consultant feels under terrific pressure to fill the gap—to make another consultation that will be more helpful, more supportive. Then she counters this wish with the thought that this would be tantamount to handing the group the spatula. The silence continues and the group seems to be wrestling now with some terrific paranoid anxieties. Whomsoever shall speak first will be killed off in some way! They will have differentiated themselves from the group by taking this momentous step and when they return there will be no place for them. They will die! If anyone should speak and if it should be in any way related to what the consultant said, they have formed a link with the bad consultant, they are in cahoots with the work of the group and thus the consultant. They have become at one with her—one of them, and they must die. The silence continues. These aforementioned terrors—of differentiation and of increased competence through joining with the task are also exciting possibilities. The struggle in the group and in the individuals continues. It is at times like these that the strength of holding environment of the group is sorely tested. Is the group confidential? Are the boundaries around the group secure? Has the consultant maintained her role in a good-enough manner? Have time boundaries been observed? Is this group a reliable object? It is as if the group is belaying off a high cliff, into empty space and, using the group as an anchor for its ropes, needs to check several times before taking the first step into thin air.

All of this is analogous to the physical containment that still allows for free movement and the eye contact the infant made in the "spatula game."

Eventually the group will fill the empty space. How this is done is of great significance. Sometimes a group member will make a "spontaneous gesture" (Winnicott, 1965a) and state for example something authentic—something from the "true self" (Winnicott, 1965a) and the group as whole will have this phenomenon to work with. For example, pursuing the "castaway" group mentioned before, a member might say something like, "I do not know why, but I felt very sad when the consultant made that last comment." Frequently, the group will respond to this silence or to a member's spontaneous gesture by fight, flight, dependency or by creating "pastimes" or "games"— perhaps by engaging in a great deal of "sound and fury" but signifying nothing. Or the group goes flat and dead, as if the meaning had been scooped out of it. The flatness and deadness, however seems largely outside the awareness of the group. The emptiness moves from being "emptiness revealed" to "emptiness concealed" (Hazell 1984b) and the group shifts from the possibility of the "type A" communicative field of Langs (1978) to the unconscious violence and interpersonal pressuring of the "type B" field or the dull wasteland of the "type C" field. The latter two fields can be understood as defensive reactions to the emergence in awareness of the experience of emptiness.

The type A communicative field is a field in which the hermeneutic function is active and disciplined, not inactive, as it is in the type C field or undisciplined, as it often is in the type B field. The type A field corresponds to the "transitional space" of Winnicott. Therefore the capacity to function in the transitional space involves the capacity to tolerate the revelation of the experience of emptiness. The logic here is consistent insofar as emotional growth relies on the capacity to participate in the transitional space (the capacity to play, according to Winnicott) and emotional growth is directly correlated with the intensity and frequency of experienced levels of emptiness. Winnicott has stated that in order to do psychotherapy, one has to wait for the patient to develop the capacity to play, but that sometimes one has to wait for a very long time. One of the reasons one has to wait for so long if that the symbolic activity involved in the play has to develop in and of itself; another is that the exercising of the hermeneutic function involved in play will reveal painful memories and the associated affect, another, and this is the focus in this paper, is that play involves the revelation of emptiness, in several ways. To this point in this paper the emptiness experienced as one initially encounters the transitional space has been the focus. This is perhaps analogous to the emptiness of the poet who gazes at the empty page or the composer who must hear silence before the true melody can emerge, or the dancer who stands still before the spontaneous gesture arrives. It is perhaps very close to Keats' notion of "negative capability."

If the therapist is the guardian and champion of the true self and the true self is realized through the transitional space, and the transitional space involves working through the awareness of the experience of emptiness, then the therapist needs an intricate knowledge of the experience of emptiness and the many wily tactics aimed at destroying the emptiness before there has been an opportunity for the spontaneous gesture and its correlate, the true self to emerge.

A word on floundering. That which I have written before should not be taken as advocating letting clients flounder uselessly for extended periods of time. The infant in Winnicott's example was supported and encouraged while encountering the moment of hesitation. The empty page in the squiggle game (Winnicott 1971) is confronted by both the child and the therapist and the transitional space is encountered by both the therapist and the client, rather as two improvisational actors using the "yes and" technique confront an unscripted expanse of time and space. I recall holding a small baby only a few weeks old. As I held him he would relax for a while and then, after a minute or so, he would push for some free space. I complied and gave him more room to maneuver. At first he enjoyed this, flexing and waving his arms and legs around in the sort of semi-controlled fashion of the infant. Then, bit-by-bit, he became distressed, as if it was too much for him. He needed containment and I would hold him closer in, snuggling him. He relaxed and seemed to enjoy this for a few minutes and then he started pressing outwards and the cycle repeated several times. I learned a lot in those few moments about the need to be contained and held and the need to be let go and experience empty space. Another common experience with children when one asks them to draw a picture on a sheet of paper that is "too big" and when they need help filling in seems analogous. Sometimes the gaps left by the therapist are too great, or the "referential distance" is too great and the client does not encounter an optimally calibrated experience of emptiness but one that is overwhelmingly large—one that is a "horrid empty space" as Balint (1968) has described and which overtaxes the integrative and creative capacities of the client's ego. They then migrate into type C or B communicative fields. The derivatives offered by the client and the vicissitudes of the client's symptoms should inform the therapist as to when this is the case.

For example, Celia, a woman in her fifties with markedly schizoidal features would frequently, in response to a comment aimed at making contact with a childhood trauma, become very distant and stare vacantly into space. After a while she would make eye contact with me and raise her eyebrows as if to say "So? What next?" Upon exploration, we would discover that she had drifted off and lost contact with the original thoughts and feelings and had often quite forgotten what had happened. (Much in the way her mother had "drifted off.") I believe that in this case had I not intervened Celia would have continued drifting in an empty sea. This was not the relaxed "unintegration" that Winnicott speaks of, that usually feels quite benign, warm and productive. This feeling with Celia was more infused with paranoid fantasies and a real jumpiness, for example in response to noises coming from outside. In this flat, gray, limitless ocean that Celia found herself drifting in, I was willing to interpose myself, in a not-too-provocative manner to help demarcate a transitional zone where we could begin to "play." At first this was really constricted, later, it involved quite elaborate and intense guided fantasy.

By way of comparison, I recall Lavender, an African American woman in her early twenties who was working through issues with an overbearing, cantankerous and explosive father. She would come into sessions and seem to slide into a reverie, almost like a cat snoozing in the sun—not saying much, and when she did say things they seemed to come out of the blue—"I never noticed how small your feet are until now" or, "I am so tired of being a "successful young Black Woman!" I might respond and she would say "Hmmm," and resume her reverie. The emotional tone was decidedly pleasant, relaxed. The emptiness was there—not stretched close to breaking point as in the groups described at the beginning of this section, not overwhelming as with Celia, but optimally-sized ("Just right!" Goldilocks might assert). In this way Lavender was able to make use of the experience, to float and become unintegrated. Fortunately I had read enough Winnicott at this point in my career to sustain this experience of emptiness and let her be—to let the impulses arise from the unconscious to be experienced, and to allow the ego to organize around this excitement and to thus be linked with the true self.

The true self can be understood as the opposite of "character," if we use character in the sense implied by Reich (1933) where it takes up the same meaning as Winnicott's "false self." This opposition is also equivalent to that of Perls (1965,1973) discrimination between "character" (that which is rehearsed and done for others) and "personality" (which is flexible, authentic and spontaneous). Character, or the false self is that which is erected in response to impingements from the environment. It is rigid and brittle, phobic and paranoid. Character, resulting, as it does from trauma finds it hard to play in any but the most ritualized of ways or in a manner that is sado-masochistic. In this regard, character can only occupy the type B and C fields of Langs (1978). Personality, or the true self is spontaneous and flowing—it is close to the very concept of "flow" described by Csikszentmihalyi (1990). The true self defies definition. In a Zen like paradox, if one feels one has defined the true self one has not; that which is defined is not the false self, for definition implies fixedness and rigidity. However, as therapists we must, as guardians of the true self, recognize it when we see it. Perhaps the negative definition will help us. The true self is that aspect of the self that is **not** erected in response to impingements from the environment.

Thus, a therapist interested in acting as a guardian of the true self must ensure that he is not impinging upon the other in such a fashion as to create encrustations of false self-adapted to the intrusions of the therapist. Frequently this will mean the leaving open of empty spaces into which the true self may flow. In addition, of course, the therapist has to be aware of the fact that even when he or she does not impinge there are plenty of internalized objects in the client's mind that are quite equal to the task. These will either act within the client's own mind as an internal saboteur or will be actively projected into the therapist where they make take up residence—perhaps to do mischief with the therapist or, should the therapist act out countertransferentially, to do mischief, once again with the client. These processes are, of course extremely "sticky" and require a great deal of therapeutic acumen.

The following clinical example illustrates well how slippery and paradoxical these processes can be and how, if one is not careful, one can end up doing years and years of "false self therapy"—the kind of therapy fairly often met with, where the client has worked very hard and long but feels that real change in their core has taken place. The clinical management of the experience of emptiness lies in the back of such cases.

Clara was a forty-year-old white woman. Professionally accomplished, she presented suffering from "binge eating," depression and low self-esteem. She was divorced from a rather sadistic-sounding man and was vigorously seeking a partner, mostly without luck; the men she ended up with tended to be marginal, somewhat schizotypal fellows, often still attached to their mothers and incapable of sustaining a long term relationship with a woman. She would tend to empathize deeply with the pain these men often carried within them and gained their initial affection with motherly ministrations and caring. About three months into the relationship she would start to assert herself in some way and the relationship would fall to bits, with much pain and suffering on her part. The men seemed to be more mystified and distant and they moved on with seeming ease to the next relationship.

Very early on in the treatment, I became aware of a rather disturbing countertransference reaction—one that trained clinicians reading this case will have, no doubt, already guessed. Clara was an "easy" client. I looked forward to sessions with her as an easy hour. She talked actively. She had plenty to work on. She was undemanding, non-hostile, smiling, attentive and a "good worker." She did not resist explorations into her dreams or unconscious motivations. Why then, wasn't she getting better? Many clients will themselves ask this question of the therapist in fairly short order, but not Clara. Eventually she might make a passing comment about how much therapy she had had and how little change she had seen, but this was something she supposed: a) that she had to live with; and, b) that was mostly her fault anyway. This foray made into the negative transference, she would quickly get back to work. Bion felt that if there was not some fear in a session then nothing was happening. For me the fear is to do with exploring the unknown. It is to do with emptiness—the void. I was experiencing no fear in sessions with Clara; therefore this was all about character, all about false self. The key, as usual was to go back to childhood. Clara's mother (that is, of course, the internalized mother, the one presented to the therapist in sessions) was rigid, narcissistic, explosive, overweening, controlling and insulting. Her mother's narcissism was of the sort one finds at the edge of psychosis, brittle, delusional and close to megalomaniacal in its magical sense of omnipotence. Clara had, with typical intuition and empathy organized herself in such a way as to prevent her mother from going psychotic and had developed many of the talents of an excellent psychiatric nurse. No wonder I felt so good in sessions! But of course none of that would help her get better. Several interpretations along the lines that she was adapting herself to me as if I was a near psychotic mother, and that she was avoiding "stressing" me too much in much the same way she had to avoid stressing her mother lodged well in her mind, for she was extremely bright. But this did not solve the problem. Once she knew what she was doing and what the way out was she confronted emptiness. She had no idea of how to be herself, free from ministering to the needs of a borderline other. When she tried, there was a vacuum. I term this position "the edge of character," for if Clara were to act differently, it would be "out of character," not like her at all. She would be all at sea, and, besides, beyond character, she only experienced empty space.

It is tempting for the client at this juncture to find some way to justify going back to the old ways—to cook up a crisis, to miss sessions, to pick a fight on some other issue. Reich (1933) and Lowen (1972) were masters at showing how the character, once it softens in one domain (in their language, one region of the body) will be compensated for by a rigidification in another area of the body so as to maintain the status quo.

It is tempting also for the therapist to introduce some routines that the client may use as a prosthetic device of some sort—to graft on as another false self, to hurriedly fill the painful and distressing sense of helpless emptiness. By analogy, for years the prairies of the Midwest of the United States of America were regarded as empty wasteland. Then came a stronger steel plough and what was wasteland became a breadbasket. Similarly, a client may be best served if they can discover from their true selves an authentic response to the empty space outside their character. This takes the form of them doing something that surprises themselves, perhaps even astonishes themselves. With Clara, for example it showed in a series of spontaneous confrontations with others. None of this went smoothly. I believe that the true self is very often inconvenient. (I recall Winnicott's axiom that health is always more challenging than illness, by which he meant, I believe, that ritualized false self-activity can be easily contained by character and bureaucracy, while spontaneous action often presents us with a problem. No more is this the case than in true love; witness the inconvenience of Romeo and Juliet)

It is around this nexus of ideas that object relations theory integrates with the theory of positive disintegration. The emergence of the true self is intertwined with the experience of spontaneity and astonishment at oneself. This latter is the harbinger of level three of Dabrowski's theory where the third factor (autonomous choice) emerges and there is a felt discrepancy between the true self and the false self. I refer the reader to Dabrowski's work for a detailed exposition on the many other manifestations of this level of emotional development, for it provides us with an excellent road map into this territory. Note also the shift away from the "other directedness" of level two of Dabrowski's theory towards the autonomy of level three. We can see this even in the very brief presentation of Clara's case. It is also predicted that as the individual moves from level two to three, the nature of the emptiness shifts from a "blank void" to a more existentially tinged emptiness as the individual, to borrow Allport's felicitous term, goes through the process of "coming into being" (Allport, 1955).

Another case illustration will serve to emphasize the importance of the phenomenon of being at the edge of one's character—the phenomenon of being at the outer limits of the "performance envelope" defined by one's character. Much psychotherapy occurs well within these boundaries of the envelope of character. Much short-term therapy is achieved without addressing issues of lifelong, across-situation adjustment, but frequently clients want to change themselves at the level of character and may enter therapy with this view in mind or "re-contract" for work at this level once the initial ego-syntonic problems have been resolved. Isaac, a white man in his early forties was going through the throes of a classic mid-life crisis as described by Levinson (1978) when he presented for therapy. He was in a state of despair. He hated the way he had lived his life thus far, which had been basically aimed at pleasing his parents—a harshly critical father and a subtly undermining mother—and he hated his life as it was now, plagued by depression, shame and self loathing. The old had died but the new had not yet been born. He seemed to have a good grasp of the problem on a theoretical level. He had spent much of his life placating others and his internal critics and had developed into a quiet, bookish man, shy, retiring and intellectual; all this despite his working-class origins.

He was filled with rage at a life of unfulfilled dreams: isolated, unmarried, childless and with no major career or creative achievements, he felt like killing himself. He had an idea of how he wanted to be—robust, energetic, social and assertive—but those qualities were beyond him—outside of his character. It was as if he went into the computer files labeled "Vigorous and Joyful Self Assertion," hit the button "Open" but got the message, "Files Empty", and there he sat with the blankness yawning in his face. Empathic resonance with the client around this emptiness, a resonance that neither pushes to one side or the other of this boundary around the character, can, I believe, create the optimal environment for the spontaneous gesture. I recall trips I have taken. How I would eagerly and excitedly plan for them and await the day of departure, and how somehow, on the morning of the day to leave, the desire would slip away into indifference. The wish to go would only be a memory. I would go anyway, hoping that the excitement would meet up with me on the road; it usually did, but the first few steps were usually taken with indifference into emptiness, as if I had dissociated from the part of myself that was going on this adventure. Recollections such as these, although I might not share them with the client (that is another related topic) would help me gain empathic contact with the individual at the edge of their character, at the edge of what Perls calls, "the fertile void."

Emptiness, Transitional Objects and Autistic Objects

The true self emerges in the play of the transitional space. Note that I did not say that the true self is in the transitional place; merely that it is symbolized in the play that occurs and can only occur in the transitional space. The true self is, by definition, beyond definition, but it is nonetheless symbolized in an ever-evolving form in symbolic activity. Symbolic activity is relational. The transitional space is relational. It occupies the space in between self and other. The earliest activity in the transitional space, namely the creation of the transitional object, is itself a representation of a primordial relationship of self and other, perhaps incorporating elements of self and placental-mother.

Lacan's notion of *the torus* (Lacan, 1953) is useful here insofar as it posits that the self has a center of gravity outside of its volume. The self can be seen as having the shape of a doughnut where the center of gravity is located in the center of the hole. The mass of the doughnut is analogous to the interpersonal relationship and the hole corresponds to the transitional space, what Langs (1978) refers to as the area of illusion.

Locating the self (or more accurately, symbolic representations of the self) in this intermediate, interstitial region, between "self and others" as a virtual image in virtual space creates a self-sense that is radically different from a psychology that locates the self in other regions. Typical, and fairly conventional variations on this theme locate the self in the view of others (other directedness) or maintain an essentialist view of the self (what I like to call the "Popeye" theory. Popeye, the sailor man, claimed in his theme song, "I am what I am"). Many people are struggling with these issues of the "location of the self," and are unable to decide on which theory to live by. This struggle is typical of the confusion, ambivalence and ambitendency found at levels two and three of Dabrowski's theory. When an individual is certain that the self is located the views of others or is certain that the self is located in essential qualities alone, this would correspond to Dabrowski's level one of emotional development. This certainty is also a manifestation of the reliance on "autistic objects" (Tustin, 1972). Thus the course of development involves a movement from the use of autistic objects towards and through the use of transitional objects and into the transitional space.

Superficiality is the annulled passionate distinction between hiddenness and revelation.   It is the revelation of emptiness…

> Søren Kierkegaard,
> *Two Ages*

Chapter 3

REMORSE AND RESISTANCE

The emotion of remorse is one of the most painful emotions the human being has to bear. So terrible is it that it will frequently block the pathway to growth. What is the feeling of remorse? It is a complex emotion, comprised of sadness, regret, anguish, loss and despair. In many ways it is similar to the "existential guilt" of Sartre (1956) and Camus (1965). It is often preceded, in the therapeutic process, by what I have come to call the "terrible moment." The moment is a "realization" in the sense that Bion (1977) uses the word, that is in the sense that there is the distinct feeling in the therapist that a "wild thought" that has been wandering the forests of the unconscious has just entered the realm of the conscious. The "terrible moment," when it is related to the emotion of remorse takes the form of the therapist having a realization, often sudden, that may take the form of, "and it has always been that way," or, "all your life you have been depressed and felt unwanted," or "you have always felt unwilling to make contact with other people for fear they will engulf you" and so on. The individual has a terrible recognition of some self-sabotaging behavior, or of some psychic pain that has crippled them or hampered their progress or that they have had to live with for long periods of time. These realizations are connected with choices that have been made that have lead sometimes to disastrous consequences. The anguish of these realizations is exquisite. If the therapist has them first, and on many occasions, of course, the therapist for reasons of countertransference will resist being open to these realizations, then she is in the dilemma of whether or how to share them with the client, for to do so is to uncover psychic pain that has previously been kept under wraps.

Once the material has been shared with the client or if the client comes to the realization himself or herself—then they have their own "terrible moment" There is the exceedingly complex experience of psychic pain. On the one hand, there is the remembering of the trauma, be it acute or cumulative and on the other hand, and this is the focus here, there is the terrible feeling of remorse—that the trauma contributed to a "life unlived." One of my favorite therapists used to say, "An unexamined life is not worth living, but an unlived life is not worth examining." A corollary of this argument would be that an unlived life is not worth living, and here we arrive at the element of deep despair in the feeling of remorse. "I have not lived." Add to this the feeling of existential guilt," I have committed the crime of not living," and a feeling of despair, "and I shall never live."

Clients and therapist alike wish to avoid painful feelings like these. Therapists may feel like they are causing unnecessary pain to clients and thus not uncover feelings of remorse, or even try to talk the client out of their remorse with hopeful and uplifting comments. If this is done the client is left alone with their remorse and with the self-hatred and despair that are part of it. Perhaps the patterns of self-defeating behavior or depression and despair persist. Perhaps both the client and the therapist see the client as

143

resisting or as a chronic case—a "help-rejecting complainer" and no forward movement occurs. My belief is that only by opening up the complex of the feeling of remorse can forward movement be made.

Often when the remorse is touched upon, there is the feeling in the room that a guilty secret has been broached, that one is embarking upon sacred and private territory. This is connected with deep feelings of shame about being in a position of powerlessness to live one's life fully or to have control (even if only in fantasy) in an assertive manner over one's future. All of these feelings, and related bodily states must be resonated with empathically by the therapist if the feeling of remorse is to be worked through and if the client is to move beyond the remorse, the focus of which is the past, and into the here and now and the future.

A quick and relatively simple example comes to mind. I was working with a group for ten weeks. They did relatively little work, despite the interventions of the co-therapists and myself. They were biding their time, playing it safe. Eventually it came time for the group to take a few weeks' break. As is often the case, the group, during the last session started to evaluate its progress. Fairly soon it became apparent that not much had happened, no matter what template you used to evaluate the group. The reality of this was stark and painful for all the members, and gradually the group slid into the feeling of remorse, at first on the relatively small scale regarding what opportunities had been missed in this group, but then, falteringly, into the larger issues of life at large—of missed opportunities, risks not taken, intimacies not shared, help not offered—*life not lived.*

As these feelings emerged, the group fell into a slump of depression. It was the mournful, low-key feeling I have come to associate with the depressive position of Klein (1946). It was as if the group had used itself, its life-affirming possibilities and, by extension, life itself, badly. It had mutilated the possibility of life and now was sitting with, attempting to contain this terrible fact, this awful realization that something had been given to them and they had destroyed it. These feelings were almost unbearable for everyone concerned. An interpretation by the therapist along the lines just spelled out seemed to help somewhat and the group towards the end seemed to resolve to live a little more fully and deeply when the group re-convened. We shall see.

Another example. Bridget, after ten years of therapy, reaches the point where she confronts "the chasm." This chasm is an internal psychological experience of great terror, dread and foreboding. It occurs first in the therapy as a metaphor, but then takes hold with the power of a waking dream. She is at one side of the chasm, with me at her side and on the other is a terrified little girl, sitting on a ledge that is crumbling away by the minute. The situation is desperate and urgent. If the little girl is not rescued soon she may die, with dire consequences for Bridget, who, at 52 years of age is seeking rejuvenation, an activation of her girlish parts that were left behind in the debris of a traumatic and chronically cold childhood. For several months the therapy focused on the painstaking "rescue mission" carried out by the therapist and Bridget, in collaboration. (In

Fairbairnian terms, this was the rescue of the "libidinal ego" (Fairbairn, 1952) or of the "regressed ego" of Guntrip (1969)). I shall not spell out the details of this phase of therapy, but shall mention that the work of Winnicott (1965a) on the functionality of therapeutic regression was of enormous assistance, and that at every step of the way a ghoulish mother would emerge in all sorts of slippery forms to undermine the little girl's forward progress. One key element of the pain Bridget underwent in this therapeutic progression was the excruciating pain of remorse—of the life that had been unlived by the terrified and lonely little girl on the ledge. In addition to the horror of the internal situation, there was the anguish of the life unlived when parts of the self are left incommunicado for fifty-plus years. Had Bridget been unable to bear this pain, I think forward movement would have been stalled.

What, then was the key to her being willing to endure this pain? The answer is not a new one. Hope and trust. Trust that the therapist will stay in contact during the regressive crisis, that she will not "go away" physically or emotionally and the hope for a more complete life once the rescue operation is complete. This hope comes partly from the therapist who in their very being communicates the worthwhileness of living and who will state their confidence of success, although these statements are usually fraught, as they should be given the gravity of the situation, with considerable concern and anxiety.

Bridget's mother took on many terrifying forms throughout the "escape" of her "little girl." She clung on tenaciously and seemed to show up at every turn— sometimes she took on the form of a howling wind, or a large shape that blocked the path, or a man, or as tentacles around the little girl's ankles. She would not let go. Of course, neither could Bridget let go of her mother. The external ("real") mother was a little sick old lady, feeble and fragile, living thousands of miles away. Not so the internal mother, to whom Bridget was stuck like glue. The point is this. Remorse involves identification (and of course for Fairbairn, all identification is pathological) with a "bad object." To cling to the remorse is to cling to the bad object. To work through the remorse is to free oneself from the "tie that binds" and to live more freely on one's own terms. Thus the working through of remorse entails the working through of pathological object-ties. This is always resisted—usually because of the fear of abandonment by the object. (One can be abandoned by an internal object); not infrequently by guilt and hope that one will one day remedy the internal relationship or gain some measure of control. These forms of guilt and hope impede development. Sometimes the relinquishing of the pathological object tie is resisted because of the fear of being (Tillich, 1952) or because of pleasure anxiety (Lowen, 1972).

Remorse is frequently the result of repeated behaviors—"I realize I have always sabotaged my relationships." "I now see that I have constant run-ins with authority figures"—and so on. These repeated behaviors are driven by the repetition compulsion. Thus to reach the emotion of remorse is to uncover the repetition compulsion and to start the arduous work of releasing oneself from the clamp of the past and to begin to live one's life anew—to get a fresh start. Remorse depends on remembering. Remembering, as

Freud points out (1914) is the precondition for working through. Remembering will take the place of repeating. The journey from repetition to liberation from repetition traverses Bunyan's (1678) "slough of despond": remorse. "Cheering up" will not do. In fact it can be construed, in these instances, as an example of manic flight from the depressive work of mourning.

The individual, prior to remorse is remorseless, a close companion to ruthlessness. Perhaps the remorseless individual, or the remorseless parts of the individual go at things with a vengeance. There is a lack of what Winnicott calls "ruth." Sectors of the self and other are split off, unacknowledged, parts are not "joined to the main" [to link to John Donne's meditation (1624)]. To a greater or lesser extent, the individual is in the paranoid-schizoid position (Klein, 1946). The emotion of remorse is characteristic of the depressive position. If the individual can tolerate the integration inherent in the depressive position [and Klein (1946)] amply illustrates the reasons why this may not be the case) the array of depressive emotions emerges—guilt, concern, devotion, the need to repair and, I would add, remorse—remorse over having bitten the hand that fed you and remorse over having destroyed parts of oneself.

In the absence of remorse, the individual is left with fantasies of dead or dying objects of self-parts that might retaliate for the harm meted out to them, and the paranoia and its *sequalae* unfold.

In my work on the experience of emptiness (Hazell, 1984a, 1984b, 1989), I found that the experience of emptiness was a sign of emotional growth *in statu nascendi*. The experience of emotional growth was intertwined with this painful experience. Individuals who shied away from this experience and filled the void with action, drugs, noise, violence, self-inflation ultimately robbed themselves of the possibility of self-transformation. It would seem that a similar argument could be made for the experience of remorse. There is something sad, and yet so human about this. Is it any wonder that our emotional and psychological development is so painfully slow when the very process of growth itself involves such gaping pain? Does it not speak to the intense need for support systems around these painful emotions and the development of a language to help chart these "dark continents" of the mind?

And since the possession of qualities presupposes that one takes a certain pleasure in their reality, all this gives us a glimpse of how it may all of a sudden happen to someone who cannot summon up any sense of reality—even in relation to himself—that one day he appears to himself as a man without qualities.

> Robert Musil,
> *The Man Without Qualities*

Rien n'est si insupportable à l'homme, que d'être dans un plein repos, sans passions, sans affaires, sans divertissement, sans application.

Il sent alors son néant, son abandon, son insuffisance, sa dépendance, son impuissance, son vide.

> Pascal,
> *Pensées*

Chapter 4

RESISTANCE TO WORKING IN THE HERE AND NOW

It was at a Group Relations Conference in the "Tavistock Tradition" (A.K. Rice 1965), that the question arose, "What is the relation of the task to the here and now?" It was one of those beguiling yet provocative questions only a beginner can ask, and that at the same time, throws the experienced worker back on their heels, looking for an answer. In a "Tavy" or group relations conference the explicit task is to examine the group process in the here and now. To engage in this task is enormously subtle, somewhat akin to a stream of water from a tap, it is clearly there, but try to grab hold of it! The examination of psychosocial flow is perhaps comparable in complexity to the examination of fluid flow in hydrology or traffic science. However, that is the task. Groups, as Bion has amply documented (Bion 1961), have enormous difficulty staying on this task and generate many ways of straying from this with other "tasks" that are far from the primary task of examining the here and now. These anti-work activities fall into Bion's three "basic assumptions" of dependency, fight-flight and pairing (Bion, 1961).

Groups engage in a wide array of "there and then" activities as if in full flight from the here and now task—nostalgia, interviewing, curing, travelogues, storytelling, "Bible making," scapegoating, planning, theorizing, "seminizing" (behaving as if one were in a seminar), adjudicating and so on. Bion's notions regarding the difficulties groups and individuals have in learning from experience are of great help in understanding the intensity of this flight from examining the here and now. Clearly some forces other than the pure and simple difficulty of the task are required to explain such a persistent avoidance. Difficulty alone would only push so far and for so long. The notion that when one learns from experience there is an especially strong pairing between elements of self and object and between elements of experience and that in the psychotic parts of the personality this can lead to "attacks on linking" that pre-emptively and enviously undo any attempt at connection seems especially powerful in explaining the force of this avoidance. The ersatz "learning" that is part and parcel of the above-mentioned litany of avoidances of the task does not involve such a powerful linkage and thus does not evoke the same powerful attack on linking. In my mind this attack on linking is the same as the activity of the "antilibidinal ego" or "internal saboteur" of Fairbairn (1952). Learning from experience is powerfully object-related and saturated with object-seeking libido. To activate it and realize it is to stir up the wrath of the internal saboteur. Observed in groups, this could play out with one individual, the designated "work leader," becoming scapegoated by sectors of the group that take up the role of the antilibidinal ego—in extreme cases splintering the thought and learning of the group until it seems to become thought-disordered.

Another resistance to working the here and now is more prosaic. In great swaths of this culture, individuals and groups attempt to gain control over their experience by "locking into" secondary process thought. Much of here and now work involves making contact with primary process phenomena where the sense of mastery and control is subjugated to that which is slippery and spontaneous.

This experience is often tied in with a sense of shame since in our culture there is a strong agenda towards planful controlled activity. There is erotization of cognition, logic and linear time concepts and a shame-saturated fear of that which is more "primitive." Thus, a flight from the here and now work. This dynamism is often encountered in here and now group work as individuals insist that the here and now phenomena they encountered were not "real" but were the result of a manipulation by the staff—a grand experiment that created psycho-social artifacts. (Of course, this is an accurate perception if the staff of the conference has been unduly provocative or if there has not been "good enough management").

A further response to the question ("Why is it so difficult to work?") seems to be suggested by the work of Heidegger (1927). For Heidegger, the experience of being is inextricably bound up by conceptions of time. In our everyday sense of being we are strapped by "concerns," by projects that involve both past and present. Our common or garden sense of being is thus derived from historicity and futurity—our sense of being is derived from "there and then" aspects of time. These aspects of time are part of our "thrownness" as we are further captured by social consensus (the "they") that further holds us outside of the here and now. The payoff of this is a sense of being, albeit and inauthentic sense of being that has some semblance of continuity through time. We feel that we, like others exist in time—a time defined by our concerns and our care about these concerns. We have a way of defining ourselves as beings in time— often in a conventionalized fashion. There is a sort of comfort in this—it affords some sense of "going on being," to use Winnicott's apt phrasing.

Heidegger points out, however, that there are "moments of vision," which he labels "ecstatic" states when the individual is not fully captivated by the historical and futural conceptions of being (of a sense of being based on what I was and what I shall be) but of an authentic being free from historicity and futurity—a being, I would argue that exists in the here and now, outside of the historicity and futurity of "conventional" notions of being. (Heidegger uses the term "ecstatic" not so much in the sense of ecstatic joy, but more in the sense of "outside" or beyond" which is closer to the root meaning of the word.) It is clear that we are close to the core of existential thinking in so far as the notion of "the essence of one's being" is probably based upon one's history and one's conception of the future, i.e. upon time. Subtract time, history and future and we are left with no essence. Thus "existence precedes essence." Essence of being is constructed and defined by one's rendition of history, by one's shaping of historical narratives and by one's construction of the future—where one locates oneself in an arc of "time." But this essence is a construction.

Back to "Tavy" conferences and "working in the here and now." Viewed from this "Heideggerian" perspective, the resistance is seen in a new light. When we ask others to work in the here and now, we are asking them to relinquish their moorings in time, and thus to relinquish their existential anchorages. This is a risk. It was argued above that the sense of going on being is established through the conventional means of "projects" that locate our being in time (and thus space). To shift into the "here and now" is to relinquish this and partake, at least potentially, in *"ecstasies"* or *moments of vision.*

Whence then the sense of being? Whence the secure sense of "going on being"? This is the risk. I hypothesize:

a) In groups where the "holding environment"(Winnicott, 1965) is felt to be inadequate, there will be a resistance to entering into the here and now work because the risk to going on being will be too great.

b) In groups where the capacity to link primary and secondary process is impaired or absent or inadequate, there will be little or no venturing forth into the here and now because the threat of taking a no-return trip into the here and now is too great—the threat to "going on being" is intolerable.

c) In groups where the capacity to "metabolize" the here and now process is too great; where the "group as mother" or the consultant staff is "incontinent" (Bion 1977), there will be reluctance to engage in here and now work for fear of losing the sense of an easy return to "going on being."

d) In groups where there is a reluctance to work in the here and now, there will be a consequent tendency to scapegoat certain individuals to carry the terrifying "unthinkable anxiety" of a no-return trip into an ocean of "non-being" with no land ever to come into view again. At the same time this scapegoated individual will be seen to contain certain visions of reality others are excluded from, a tacit recognition of the "moments of vision" this individual contains to an unbearable degree.

What has been argued in the last part of this paper is that here and now work in groups requires that individuals relinquish a conventional sense of being that is based on history and futurity. In addition, the sense of going on being is established by the adequacy and attunement of the holding environment. If the holding environment is secure and true, then here and now work may proceed, with the participants secure in the knowledge that they are firmly attached to conventional senses of being. If it is not secure and true then participants will wisely not embark in the adventure of here and now learning.

Medieval Irish mystics at times considered it a duty to God to set sail in a small boat into the vast empty, uncharted ocean—trusting their fate to God. Most sailors, however, seem to require good charts, clocks, compass, sextant, safe harbor, perhaps even the access to a radio and global positioning satellites.

It is getting late

Shall we ever be asked for?

Are we simply

Not wanted at all?

W.H. Auden,
The Age of Anxiety

Chapter 5

EMPTINESS AND THE GROUP

In this chapter the focus will be on the various forms and causes of the experience of emptiness as they occur in group settings, first in the small therapy or self-study group (with a membership typically ranging from 5 to 12 persons), and secondly in the larger group, (with a membership ranging from 25 to 130 persons).

The experience of emptiness manifests itself not only in the life of the individual, but also in the life of groups. In the course of events outside of therapy, self-study and educational settings, this emptiness is usually obscured by a wide array of operations and activities, many taking the form of the "social defense mechanisms" described and documented amply by Menzies (1960). In therapy groups and other groups aimed at support, psychological education, the experience of emptiness at a group level can be more readily seen, especially where the structure of the group is such as to allow its emergence. It has been my consistent experience, working with groups in a style heavily influenced by the "Tavistock tradition" (Coleman and Bexton 1975, Coleman and Geller 1985, Bion 1961) that the experience of emptiness has always figured prominently in the life of the group and that the resolution of this experience has been an essential ingredient of the group's evolution and growing complexity. I hypothesize further that group processes that interfere with the emergence and ultimate resolution of the experience of emptiness can, under many conditions hamper the development of the group. Viewed from this perspective, the management of the group can be understood from the perspective of the management of the experience of emptiness. At one extreme, if one phobically avoids the experience of emptiness in the group, say through "overstructuring" the educational experience, leaving no gaps into which the group can create its own meaning, then growth is hampered. At the other extreme, if one leaves too many "horrid empty places" in the structuring of the group (to use Balint's felicitous phrase, 1968), then one runs the risk of the group becoming overwhelmed by the experience of emptiness and taking recourse to the above -mentioned social defense mechanisms, closing down, ceasing to do psychological work and consequently, growing less. These broad principles apply to all groups, however, the dynamics of large and small groups are so different that this chapter is divided into two sections—one examining emptiness in the small group and one examining this experience in the large group.

Emptiness in Small Groups

The following has been, for me, a frequent experience in groups. The is a sort of chatter going on about this and that—movies, vacations, classes, dreams, shoes—and then something happens; a word is uttered by someone, perhaps the therapist or consultant and the emptiness of the chatter is revealed. The uttered word perhaps was an interpretation or perhaps was associated with a powerful feeling that was hidden behind the chatter and the group experiences, in one way or another a gap—sometimes an awful gap—

between the discourse and its meaning. This results in the experience of emptiness. Frequently the group will fall into silence—sometimes a silence that will last for a psychological eternity. A metaphor that captures some of this experience is the experience I had of seeing the Grand Canyon. I got off the coach and walked across the parking lot—no sign of any canyon—just flat desert. I walked along a dusty, sandy flat path—still no canyon. I kept walking and suddenly, unexpectedly there was the tremendous vacancy of the Grand Canyon. I was stunned and spent several seconds adjusting my focal distance until I had the measure of this empty space that hit me in the chest. Where I had just experienced flatness and two dimensionality, there was now depth and stunning three dimensionality. Groups, when they fall into this type of stunned silence seem to be experiencing this type of emptiness.

Sometimes the group will adjust to the emptiness right away—this would be where what Bion calls "basic assumption work," but on many occasions the group will utilize the above-mentioned social defense mechanisms.

Viewed from this perspective working with groups can be understood as managing the intensity and degree of the experience of emptiness. At one end of the spectrum is the group that has been structured to such an extent that there is little space for the experience of emptiness and growth is hampered. At the other extreme is the group where the structure has left such large lacunae that the group has to take recourse to social defenses of its own manufacture and this also, hampers growth.

Following is a (previously cited) clinical example. A group was in session and had been talking on about this and that. Eventually a member decides that they would like to share something personal and emotionally charged. They do so, but the group does not make a lot of emotional contact with this individual and they move on to other topics. The topic that they focused on was the movie *Castaway*. I then comment that perhaps there are experiences in this group, "parts of the group" that have been cast away, and that perhaps this is as painful for the group as it was for the individual depicted in the movie. The group fell silent for quite a few minutes.

It was as if they had been stunned by the experience of emptiness. The comment revealed a gap between their discourse and its possible hidden meaning. The comment adds a dimension of meaning to their discourse. Groups react to this gap or empty space in a set of fairly predictable ways. At times the consultation is rejected out of hand. This would be analogous to not want to see the gap or space, to not wanting to see the emptiness of the discourse and to not wanting to work on the *referential gap* between the group's discourse and the interpretation. Into this category of responses would fall such utterances as, "There he goes again! Why does everything have to have a double meaning?" Quite often, however, after an initial rejection of the consultation the group will return to the ideas expressed by the consultant, often about twenty minutes later. It is almost as if the group needed this time to adjust its vision to the depth of the therapist or consultant's remark or to prepare themselves for the psychological work needed to fill the gap created by the two "takes" on the group.

It is at this point that the group starts to do its psychological work, work that I regard as analogous to the creative filling in of the transitional space that is done by the infant and the mother as described by Winnicott (1965a). The group is exercising the *hermeneutic function* described in this book, and, in so doing, is making psychological gains.

This then exemplifies the first type of emptiness as it is encountered frequently in groups. It is an emptiness created by the very act of interpretation itself, for the interpretation reveals an emptiness in the group's discourse and creates a gap—a gap between the meaning of the discourse as perceived by the group and the meaning as perceived by the consultant or therapist. A gap is also created between the very group and the therapist by virtue of this difference in "takes," and this too is experienced as an emptiness. This is the emptiness of the encounter with *l'objet grande A* of Lacan. This is the stunning emptiness involved in the encounter with *radical alterity.* The therapist, insofar as they entertain a different interpretation of events or of discourse becomes radically other than the group. This creates a space, an emptiness. This emptiness is awesome and yet also inspiring. A working group is able to utilize this alterity towards its ends. A basic assumption group attempts to eradicate this alterity through a multitude of slick defensive maneuvers.

This dynamic manifests itself in the management of the boundaries between therapist and the group. The therapist, in taking up their role differentiates themselves from the membership of the therapy group and this creates an empty space between therapist and group members. This transitional space will dilate and compress, fill and evacuate in response to the pressures operating between the group and the therapist.

A second form of emptiness that occurs in groups takes the form so brilliantly depicted in Beckett's *En Attendant Godot*. In the previously cited example of the "castaway" group we might find that the group as a whole decides that it is not a good idea for them to leave people "just hanging" or "disconnected" and that they should take concerted efforts to ensure that there is more emotional contact. "Yes, let us do that," they say. "Yes, let's" they affirm. But they do nothing. They sit in vacuous silence for perhaps twenty minutes, with nobody daring to say anything, as if there has been total paralysis of initiative. The group feels like a spaceship where the crew has been frozen for the many year's long journey to a distant galaxy, where perhaps they will be aroused from a state of suspended animation. Clinically all in the group seem in a state of blank schizoidal withdrawal. The consultant is reminded of babies lying in "isolettes" in neonatal intensive care units as the group sits in blank vacuous emptiness, not talking, not anxious, not depressed—just staring into space. There is a tremendous pull on the therapist to tickle and tease the group, to pull on them, to get them to do something—smile perhaps—but this desire is countered by the belief that to do this would only result in them complying with the desire of the therapist and thus to create a "false compliant self." Ultimately the therapist presents himself or herself as an object that is willing to connect when the group is ready and able to exercise some spontaneous initiative and waits. And, as Winnicott tells us, sometimes you have to wait a long time.

A common pattern to emerge in groups that "lapse" into this "schizoidal" form of emptiness is as follows. The emptiness results from an agreement in the group not to make emotional contact. At one level this agreement is struck because to make emotional contact is to reveal emotions in the group and this is experienced as shame; shame being experienced as a loss of control (especially of the body) in public. Another reason this "hands off" agreement is struck is because there is a belief that to make emotional contact with another only deepens the pain the other might be feeling and that this deepening of the other's pain will lead to a retaliatory attack—either by the other individual or by the whole group. Further, the emotional contact is avoided because there is a fear that the other will feel disrespected, invaded, prodded, probed or taken over by the curious one and that this will lead again to a retaliatory attack. In addition there could be a group as a whole prohibition of curiosity or of linking things together—of seeing things or of putting one and one together and that this leads to a compact of schizoidal withdrawal.

All of the above is more than enough to keep a group fused into a condition of empty isolation for protracted periods of time, and while some of these anxieties are relatively developmentally late, that is those having to do with sexual curiosity or shame over making a mess of things, many of them are extremely primitive, having to do with the "attacks on linking" described by Bion (1959). This can keep the group "stuck" in empty Godot-like spaces for long periods. Groups where this dynamic is predominant can exasperate therapists and provide many temptations to intervene and do something to stimulate activity. Therapists encountering this type of emptiness often feel worthless as their contributions are emptied of meaning. Sometimes they wish to retaliate against the group as if to punish them for not working. Any of these responses are either un- or antitherapeutic insofar as they stimulate "false-self activity," activity that only deepens the emptiness and therefore deepens the problem.

It is my opinion that groups of this nature are occurring much more frequently, owing to the massive socio-technical changes currently occurring on a Global scale.

Even as the group described above attempts to make emotional contact and fill in the voids that permeate its structure, all does not proceed smoothly. Frequently the emotional contact that group members experience can be over stimulating, and they recoil into withdrawal as if the contact is painful, in a manner similar to the recoiling of foundling-home toddlers described by Spitz (1965). The tenderness that emerges with connectedness is an *unbearable tenderness*—a tenderness saturated with the innocence of childhood—tenderness difficult to contain in language and prone to the *confusion of tongues* described by Ferenczi (1955). Here the group will struggle with the language of tenderness and the language of passion. In this confusion of tongues members may feel re-traumatized, misunderstood and retreat back to where they were before—in a state of suspended animation. It is the therapist's task to pick up on these processes—progressive and regressive.

Sometimes the emptiness is preserved by the operation in the group of a group level equivalent of Fairbairn's *internal saboteur.* At long last a tendril of the libidinal ego reaches out tentatively to another in the group only to be smashed, splintered or otherwise destroyed by a hostile hateful (perhaps envious) force in the group. This *group saboteur* can take many forms. Sometimes an individual who has a particularly good valence for this role plays it out. Sometimes a spiteful coalition will form and be maintained by the group collusively to ensure that no libidinal links will occur here. Sometimes this role is projected into the therapist, who may countertransferentially act it out. Sometimes ghosts from the past are brought in various guises to do the job. In several groups I have worked with there has been the distinct sense that the group had created a terrifying "secret police" that hovered and circled above the group and darkly and frighteningly destroyed any incipient sign of contact.

Clive Hazell

This "secret police" imago had to be "worked through" before the vacuum could be filled with spontaneity and the creation of meaning.

The "secret police" will often come equipped with a "death squad." The group sits in a paralyzed empty state in fear of getting "killed" should they do the wrong thing, and, as in a police state, all creativity is suppressed and meanings are suppressed in a paranoid anxiety that incriminating evidence will lead to one's demise. I understand this death squad as a projection of the group's own death wishes into this imaginary object that circulates among the group and its environs, sometimes fusing with actual persons and subgroups and leading then to potentially dangerous situations for the participants. I have found that consultations that refer to the death squad as comprised of these split of arts of all the group participants do help to enable the group to confront their anxieties and "move forward." As to whether these projected death wishes are resultant from a primordial "death instinct" as hypothesized by Freud and so interestingly pursued by Rosenfeld and Klein or whether they are essentially secondary "breakdown phenomena" as argued by Kohut and Fairbairn, I am still uncertain. This is still, for me, an open question, and while it is a fascinating and ultimately compellingly important, I find I am still able to do much clinical work in the face of this uncertainty.

This line of thought, involving projected death wishes, lead directly to another type of emptiness encountered in groups (and in individuals). I call it "black hole emptiness," the metaphor, being drawn from Grotstein (1994) indicates that the group creates, somewhere near its psychic center, a terrifying black hole into which all objects, entities, categories, thoughts, feelings and fantasies, disappear ineluctably without a trace, never to return, save perhaps at a very unconscious level, through some bizarre distorted wormhole in a far distant time and place, say the "tunnels under Jerusalem" or the "fires of Neptune in the distant past."

I encountered this deep *black hole emptiness* in consulting with an individual who was working with a group of detainees in a county jail. After the group had gone through several sessions and established a beginning "working routine," the group touched upon some emotionally stimulating material, faltered and then started to speak in a disjointed manner about dark sucking places that robbed one of everything. Memory was lost and vulnerable group members started to "lose it" manifesting the fragmentation prior to sliding over the *event horizon* of the black hole. The emptiness of the black hole is a different phenomenon from the persecutory silence evinced by the *death squad*—it has to do with total annihilation, while the death squad one can perhaps avoid if one simply suspends one's animation. I understand its underlying dynamic to be essentially the same; it is just the degree of intensity that is different.

The group as a whole has projected in this case, death wishes of the intensest variety into the imaginary object so that it is no longer contained by the fantasy of a death squad, it can only be contained by the metaphor/fantasy [almost amounting to a negative hallucination; see Andre Green (2001)]. The rage in the group is filled to bursting point; it is projected into the center of the room where it becomes a sucking black hole. A consultation such as this seems to capture much of these detainees' hellish moebius-strip-like dilemma.

Emptiness and the Large Group

The dynamics of large groups have been described in some detail elsewhere. Kreeger (1975) presents a useful array of articles and ideas. For this reason, this section will focus specifically on some dynamics that I have noticed occurring in large groups that contribute to the experience of emptiness.

Many writers have noted the extremely powerful regressive pull of the large group. Accompanying this regressive pull is the "return of the repressed." This return of the repressed often has a disruptive impact on the cohesion of thoughts. This absence of cohesion, this inability of the large group to think has the effect of destroying meaning (which relies upon coherence and cohesion of thought) and ultimately causes a sense of emptiness and futility. It is into this sense of emptiness and futility that a charismatic individual may insert himself or herself and take over the role of leader. The group, empty, as it is, of meaning, gratefully accepts the interpretations and ideas of this leader, since it provides some meaning, some interpretive framework. This is linked with the process Freud describes wherein the large group identifies with the leader and the group, in large part to overcome the sense of helplessness and insignificance the individual feels in the large group.

The return of the repressed, also involves the return of the repressed bad objects that return and act as a "saboteur" upon any acts of linking in the group. This process can be seen clearly in small groups when libidinal ties that might be created between persons, ideas, thoughts, memories and things are routinely attacked and enviously and self-protectively destroyed, but this action is especially virulent in the large group. It greatly contributes, in my estimation, to the experience of the large group as a very frightening and dangerous place. It is as if one is observing a combination of Fairbairn's "internal saboteur" and

Bion's "attacks on linking" all in one swoop. The net result, as predicted by both these authors, is psychotic like disintegration.

Thus, one typically observes, in the large group, a paralyzed anxiety regarding making contact, scattered, fragmented talk, splitting of affect and thought, polarized sub grouping, where on group is held to contain "all" the aggression, while another contains helpless, hapless victimization, envious attacks on those who can think or connect and endless other frightening frustrating phenomena. The net result is absence of meaning, void, emptiness, compounded by a group ethic of "thou shalt not connect."

An example of one form of this occurred in a large group where, towards the end of a conference a small group of women reported that they had been meeting very productively and enjoyably in the evenings of the conference and had drawn a number of useful insights from these "after hours" sessions. This island of "potential meaning" was then demolished. It was vigorously asserted that they had nothing to offer, that they should not conduct work outside of the conference, that their knowledge was illegitimate and they were all but outlaws of the system. The sub group gave in and lapsed into numbed silence. It was as if they had been enviously destroyed. Such envious attacks on "islands of meaning" are often directed at the consultant, who, in their interpretive role visibly construct and maintain meaning—a meaning that serves as a protectant against vacuum.

It is said, "nature abhors a vacuum." I am not so sure. Perhaps it is only humans who, most of the time, abhor a vacuum. It appears that, in the face of these vacuums or emptinesses, people are driven to *do something,* anything, at times, to rid themselves or the group of this painful feeling of emptiness. The more powerful is the void, the stronger the impulse to action, as if action will fill the emptiness. It does, for a while, but the emptiness returns, often amplified by the awareness that the action did not work to obliterate the emptiness.

Since stronger senses of emptiness will be encountered in large groups, we may predict that it is in large groups we will find a greater likelihood towards what Bion (1977) calls A6 activity, or what is elsewhere called "acting out." Acting out in other contexts is understood in a number of ways, for example, as a way of avoiding a feeling or thought or as a way of enacting in an unconscious drama, a traumatic event. Here, it is being argued that A6 activity (see Bion's grid) can be used in an obverse manner, namely to obscure the *absence* of a feeling or a thought or a meaning. Clinically, this is interesting, because it means that when one reverses the flow, and stops the acting out, what emerges is not a defended-against feeling, but the experience of emptiness, which is not a defense, but in many cases a resultant effect of the psi barriers and previously mentioned dynamics that have eroded the construction of meaning, that have hampered the hermeneutic function.

To venture causes anxiety, but not to venture is to lose one's self...and to venture in the highest sense is precisely to become conscious of one's self.

Søren Kierkegaard,
Fear and Trembling

Chapter 6

CLINICAL APPLICATIONS OF THE THEORY OF POSITIVE DISINTEGRATION

It is the purpose of this chapter to demonstrate the clinical applications of Dabrowski's theory [the Theory of Positive Disintegration (Dabrowski, 1970)], in an individual counseling setting and integrated with notions from object relations theory.

From a Dabrowskian perspective, the true self can be regarded as the hearth of the OE's, covered up to a greater or lesser extent by the defensive crust of the False Self. The counseling process can thus be conceived of as the liberation of the true self and its OE's from the much-needed yet confining cage of the false self.

Fairbairn's theory (1952) provides another template that is compatible with both Dabrowski's and Winnicott's theories. Fairbairn holds that the original pristine unified ego undergoes splitting into three interrelated object relations (OR) units—the central ego (CE) and the ideal object (IO), the antilibidinal ego (AE) and its partner the rejecting object (RO) and the libidinal ego (LE) partnered with the exciting object (EO) (a tantalizing object always just out of one's reach). To these three pairs Guntrip (1969) adds (with Fairbairn's blessing) the regressed ego—that part of the ego that retreats into deepest seclusion in order to survive trauma.

The libidinal ego is the part of the ego that strives for life and its many pleasures (Fairbairn's theory has no innate death instinct). However, under the aegis of splitting, these stirrings are met with the teasing of the exciting object or the outright sadism of the antilibidinal ego and rejecting object—what Fairbairn aptly calls the "internal saboteur." This wreaks havoc with the libidinal ego—perhaps causes the regressed ego to split off and go further underground, and cuts off energetic supply lines between the central ego that is in contact with the outside world and the libidinal ego. This leaves the individual feeling drained, demoralized and empty of meaning, like they have to screw themselves up just to face the day.

Fairbairn's libidinal ego is equivalent to Winnicott's True Self and as such, it can be seen as the hearth of the OE's. When one works with this template, one can visualize that the OR units often occur as what Ogden (1983) terms "semi-autonomous subpersonalities" interacting in the "matrix of the mind." Now the theoretical stage is set for work with clients towards the activation and liberation of the OE's.

It occurs through releasing the grip the negative introjects (the RO and EO and the AE) have on the libidinal ego and thus enabling the expression of the LE (OE's) through the CE into the outside world. This single sentence conceals a complex process that is perhaps best illustrated through a case vignette.

Carol was thin, timid, quiet, emotionally quite flat, frozen-faced, stiff bodied and shy. She worked as a secretary and was halfway through a masters degree in counseling. Her early complaint was of having trouble sleeping—she would awake with experiences of blank, contentless terror and be unable to get back to sleep. She also suffered from chronic pain in her legs and she felt that perhaps there was a psychological component to this problem.

Early on in treatment she brought in a piece of artwork she had done in a class at school. Prominent in this was a cave. When asked where she located herself in the artwork she said, "I am a smudge on the wall in the deepest part of the cave—not even on the wall, I am part of the wall." When I explored with her the fantasy of peeling herself off the wall (perhaps in retrospect ill-advisedly), she flooded with terror, closed down, blanked out and after a long silence, said, "I can't do it." Using Fairbairn's and Guntrip's theory I pointed out that part of herself (perhaps the most precious part) had been secreted in the depths of this cave where it would be safe from harm. Unfortunately, it also is out of the light of day where it will grow and realize itself. Why does it hide? Fairbairn would hypothesize an internal saboteur stemming from an unsatisfactory relationship with mother. And that in fact is what we found—her mother did not want her, had considered aborting her and would terrify her in multiple ways with sudden explosive rages, abandonments, envious attacks and unpredicted movings of house. In response, part of her self had gone down a bolt hole and another struggling part was above ground (in school, at work) but getting regularly torpedoed by negative introjects.

As a result—to introduce Dabrowski's theory—the OE activity was low and under siege.

Her physical activity was very limited, her range of sensual pleasures constricted, her emotionality flat and slow, her imagination difficult to tap into, as evidenced by the blank, contentless dreams and her intellectual curiosity often lead to feelings of intense fear and confusion so this too was restricted. The last, of course, placed serious constraints on her fluency with graduate school projects and papers.

The course of therapy was long and complex, but highlights that relate to the current theme can be summarized as follows:

Much work was done exploring the cold, frightening relationship she had with her mother, how she had internalized this relationship and how she tended to re-experience this relationship in the form of a repetition compulsion with other figures in her life— her ex-husband, her ex-therapist, her current boss. Also examined were her vigorous attempts to relive this tormenting relationship with me in the transference/countertransference situation. In this last she proved quite expert and persistent in evoking in me feelings of punitive rage with a dismissive contempt that she would aim at what I felt had been particularly contactful, meaningful and useful sessions. My response was to analyze these as projective identifications of her own negative internalization and as tests of my capacity not to retaliate as so many of her previous persons had. I believe I managed, for the most part, not to retaliate and re-traumatize, but to abstain, contain and metabolize and as I did so the transference/countertransference situation was characterized by a greater feeling of ease, humor and trust. About this time she discovered a Belgian chocolate store and started to bring me samples. As we luxuriated in the velvety bittersweet chocolate I did wonder aloud if she was offering me food so I wouldn't bite her and other such Kleinian musings (1946) but I was also gratified to see sensuality breaking through. Later came delicious home-made cookies and an increased interest in gardening.

I understood that the negative introjects had been sufficiently dissolved or neutralized so that the libidinal ego held more sway and the OE's (sensual and psychomotor) were more active.

As the strength of the negative introjects was countered and weakened through the positive developments in the transference/countertransference situation so her work at school proceeded, albeit at a torturously slow, anxiety-ridden pace.

She would freeze with blank fear at the word processor when trying to write a paper—as if the very continuity and coherence of her thoughts was being disrupted by a horrifying sadistic and demeaning internal saboteur. (In extreme cases, this is what I believe happens in many cases of thought disorder—to use Bion's terms (1959) the linking function of the libidinal ego or of the intellectual OE is attacked by the internal saboteur which has a hatred of anything that resembles a link—this results in confusional states.)

Using this analytic template we worked together for long hours to develop ways to protect the emergent efforts of the LE and its OE's. The results were slow and at times I found myself using unconventional techniques for example modeling giving her imaginary mother a good telling off—writing out for her (Carol) a list of 25 of her positive attributes (she may still carry this around in her wallet today)—but eventually she (I almost suspiciously say "we") succeeded and she graduated with her masters degree.

Another turning point came when one day I suggested a "Gestalt" activity with mother in the chair. As soon as I rotated the empty chair to face her for the classic Gestalt address she was paralyzed, frozen with terrorized silence.

Needless to say this event stunned her—evidencing as it did the freezing power of the introjected bad mother, and we ventilated and worked this experience through for months (on and off) after this.

As this examination of this terrifying aspect of her mother proceeded, her chronic pain abated in her legs (I often felt her "bad mother" "lived" in her legs) and her nightmares gained content, that is, there were entities, forms, symbols, places and so on. This I regarded as a significant forward step in her functioning, not only in terms of symbol-formation and moving from what Winnicott (1960) and Bion (1959) call psychotic unthinkable anxieties to neurotic thinkable anxieties, but also in terms of the elaboration of her imaginational OE. This meant that dream work and the therapeutic endeavors could move much more quickly.

About this time she discovered a "good person," appropriately named Angeline. Angeline was a masseuse and she had the magic touch. This discovery of a good person and permitting herself to use and relate to and take in the goodness of this relationship again furthered the aims of the libidinal ego enabling the expression of the sensual, emotional and psychomotor OE's. Such "good persons" can form useful alliances with the LE and facilitate treatment.

Similarly in the transference/ countertransference situation I was being regarded as a potentially beneficial person. She was becoming more able to make use of me—and perhaps feel gratitude— an important aspect of both the "depressive position" of Klein (1946) and of Emotional OE (Dabrowski, 1970.)

Her situation at work with a persecutory boss mirrored her nightmares of persecution, prosecution and terror and it deteriorated until she was finally laid off. She eventually found a satisfactory job (although one that did not use her full intellectual accomplishments: she had in the meantime graduated with a masters degree). This job, however, did come with a lively, supportive organizational environment and a robust, flexible non-persecutory boss, whom she grew to like and trust more and more.

At this time, she started to deepen a friendship with a recently divorced woman [a significant step, for she had never had that oh-so-important Sullivanian chum in pre-adolescence (Sullivan, 1953)] and they would go on long hikes and see movies together.

Again the emergence of the OE's—emotional and psychomotor as the object world, internal and external, changes.

A recent turning point occurred in therapy partly as a result of my having read the wonderfully evocative work by Alessandra Piontelli *From Fetus to Child.* (1992) In this work, Piontelli demonstrates through the use of ultrasound images and early childhood observations that there is a remarkable continuity from life in the womb to life outside the womb.

During one session she stopped in mid-sentence and said, "I just had a crazy feeling." I encouraged her to share it and she said she felt terrified that the room was closing in on her and that someone would burst in the door and kill her. (This last fantasy had been a recurrent one from the earliest days of therapy together—any sound at or near the door evolved a strong, terrified, startled response.)

I found myself containing a terrible thought—and wondering whether or not to share it. (Often the predicament of the therapist, I find). Finally I said, "Perhaps this is not such a crazy thought—perhaps it is more of a memory of what it was like to be in the inhospitable womb of a mother who did not want you and was thinking of aborting you."

Her reaction to this was one of initial puzzlement but after some connecting work—of room equals womb, door equals birth canal it clicked and her body seemed to visibly relax—her cheeks flushed, her eyes softened and her characteristic cold, frozen hard look melted away. To my surprise, I found myself thinking, "Goodness, she is very attractive...and warm." An unprecedented and significant libidinal fantasy and feeling in our relationship.

The consequences of the insight (if indeed it is an insight) have yet to be worked through—my intuition tells me some character armor (Reich, 1933) melted allowing for the true self to emerge. In Fairbairn's terms I would argue (as is so often the case with "schizoid" problems) that splitting went back to very early stages—in this case the womb—where even there she had to protect herself from trauma and erect a false self (Reich's character armor) in order to survive. This meant that she could not just relax and "be" she had to tighten up and "do." (Winnicott, 1960) As Winnicott points out, the ground of the true self (out of which it springs) is "being"—(unintegrated being). If this is denied the individual then the development of the true self and, by extension, the OE's is thwarted. I anticipate and await further emergence of the OE's as a result of this piece of work.

One word on the true self. It cannot be known ahead of time, by definition it is spontaneous, emergent, mysterious. In this there is wonder, awe, surprise, even fear. Space does not permit me to describe the remarkable "emergences" I have witnessed in this type of work with other clients—a car salesman who moves to realize a goal as a film cameraman, a stock trader who becomes a sports announcer, a social worker becoming a musician. While the realization of the True Self often involves subtle changes, in each of these cases, the self realization emerged as something of a surprise—sometimes an awkward, inconvenient surprise but with a promise of another chance of living on one's own terms, more really and with greater involvement of the whole self, libidinal ego, overexcitabilities and all.

I cherish my nights of despair

> Albert Camus,
> *The Myth of Sisyphus*

Chapter 7

THE EXPERIENCE OF EMPTINESS AND THE USE OF DABROWSKI'S THEORY IN COUNSELING GIFTED CLIENTS: CLINICAL CASE EXAMPLES

The ideas presented in this chapter were generated from ten years or so of therapeutic work with four clients known to be gifted and two suspected gifted clients in a private setting. The clients were identified as being gifted by their own reports of previous IQ tests (in excess of 130 in four cases) or by their having been placed in gifted programs in school (one case) or by an early entrance into college courses at age sixteen (one case). Four of the clients were female, two male. In addition, the findings here are buttressed by work with several other clients who, although not formally identified as gifted, manifested very high degrees of achievement and talent in their profession along with "clinical" manifestations of giftedness—such as an extraordinarily high speed of processing information, an ability to grasp very quickly very complex formulations, and so on.

Therapeutic work with these clients ranged from two to eight years, the mode being long-term work. I was the counselor and my therapeutic approach, although it continually evolved, is an integration of the ideas of Dabrowski (1967, 1970), Wilfred Bion (1977), W.R.D. Fairbairn (1952) and Ludwig von Bertallanffy (1968) in a ground of Rogerian listening (Rogers, 1961).

Dabrowski's Theory of Positive Disintegration

The work of Kazimierz Dabrowski is fundamental to my approach. Basically a theory of emotional development, the Theory of Positive Disintegration, or aspects of it, is delineated in a number of volumes (e.g., Dabrowski, Kawczak & Piechowski, 1970). The fullest exposition of the theory, however, is to be found in Dabrowski and Piechowski (1977). It is described in Chapter 1 of this book.

Emotional Development and Emptiness

In previous work (Hazell, 1984, 1989) I found that emotional development, in terms of Dabrowski's Theory of Positive Disintegration, is a potentiator of experiences of emptiness, when old systems of meaning, associated with the previous level of emotional development, collapse and disorganize before new integrations and meaning emerge and with them new motivational systems become active. We know that high levels of emotional overexcitability (OE), especially when paired with high levels of intellectual OE, stimulate emotional development (Robert & Piechowski, 1980; Piechowski, 1986). Putting these two findings together with the third that gifted individuals have high levels of all five OEs (Piechowski & Cunninghan, 1985, Piechowski, Silverman, Falk, 1985) we arrive at the hypothesis that gifted individuals will be prone to experiences of emptiness as their heightened OEs propel them through the levels of emotional development and while their frameworks of meaning shift and become positively disorganized.

My clinical work, although it does not bear the imprimatur of a tightly controlled study, bears out these predictions. (In the case material that follows all names and identifying information have been changed to protect confidentiality.)

Ted

Ted was a 25-year-old male suffering from "motivational paralysis." I was regaled weekly with his "takes" on a dazzlingly wide array of topics— television, entertainment, fame, poetry, politics, religion—the ideas spewed out with him barely able to complete a sentence in one area before the next emerged, overlapping, relating, contradictory—filling the room with a store of ideas.

Without Dabrowski's theory it would have been very easy to "pathologize" this outpouring as perhaps a "manic defense"—an idea of Melanie Klein (1935/1964) where clients create a chaos to conceal their pain—or perhaps it could even be interpreted as a mild to moderate thought disorder. The paralysis could be seen as a depression or as a form of "castration anxiety." Perhaps it is all of these and more—but what was most helpful for Ted was to acknowledge the "Dabrowskian dimension" of his discourse, to identify the collapse of meaning and the resultant motivational paralysis and emptiness as emotional growth *in statu nascendi*, i.e. as positive disintegration.

Despite his initial resistance to these ideas (they seemed to him to be unfairly elitist) their explanatory power was undeniable. Now his sense of isolation, his sense of having a very different slant on things, seemed to fall into place. Not only that, but his anxiety at his sense of having high potential now seemed not a "pathological narcissistic core" but some preconscious recognition that, given fortunate circumstances, he could have a lot to offer. This seemed to go some way to explain why it was so hard for him to have an intimate relationship—closeness and intimacy require a relatively stable sense of self and for Ted this was perhaps a more complicated and involved process.

If we were to integrate chaos theory (Gleick, 1987) and ideas emanating from self-organizing criticality (Bak, 1996) from the field of physics with Dabrowski, we might say that the increased flow of information, owing to the heightened OEs, creates transient states of disorganization (so-called "punctuated equilibrium states") as information accumulates beyond a certain point and the system goes through a "step function" to a new order.

Additional Therapeutic Theme

In addition to these "disorganization phenomena," I have noticed several other recurrent themes in my work with gifted and highly talented clients. Gifted individuals, by virtue of their extremely high emotional OE, experience emotional trauma very intensely [perhaps in what Bion (1977) calls a "psychotic like" fashion]. In this we may integrate Tomkins (1981) useful notion of affect as an amplifier and attenuator of information (and behavior) and hence of subjective experience. However, gifted individuals often exhibit high OEs across the board in five channels (sensual, emotional, imaginational, psychomotor, intellectual) and I believe that this leads to their very quickly and effectively representing the trauma in other modalities—movement, sensuality, imagination, and intellect.

This representation serves a quadruple function (at least):

> To "memorialize" the trauma to encode it in deep memory—to mark the incident without fully having to remember it.

> To communicate the trauma (in an encrypted form).

> To "contain" the unthinkable aspects of the trauma in images and ideas [Bion's (1977) preconceptions"].

> To disguise (obliterate) and bury (perhaps reverse) the trauma—to hide, undo, or eradicate the trauma from personal history.

Since gifted individuals have, at their disposal, a vast amount of developmental potential (or libido—

psychic energy), the effort expended along the lines of the OEs and serving the above four functions can be enormous. Thus, the gifted individual may show up at the therapist's office with a considerable "baggage" of accomplishments and with a very active process channeled through the OEs serving the above functions.

However, to the extent that obliteration or reversal of the OE activity is effective [as what Bion (1977) would call a truth barrier] clients' activity is not articulated with basic elements of their experience. That is, the trauma has not been fully integrated—its significance is being disavowed while being recognized and memorialized, that is "remembered" in symbolic form only. The client thus feels an emptiness, an inner void, as if he was not all there and did not fully participate in life, even though from the outside there appears to be a lot of activity and involvement.

Don

As an example, Don, a talented actor, lost a father in very early childhood. In early sessions this loss was presented with very little accompanying feeling—what was presented was a helter-skelter life of parties and work and partnering—such busyness that it was difficult even to fit counseling into the crazy quilt patchwork of his life. His life appeared full, creative, burgeoning with promise of future success. A recent relationship had just been given up on—mysteriously, it had petered out, like a river disappearing into the empty sands of the desert. But again, little feeling was demonstrated—even though descriptions of the value of the relationship betokened a considerable loss. Meanwhile the parties continued and the enormous outpouring of creative activity—Don was living, working and playing hard—but still something was missing. He would sometimes catch himself speaking and think, "How distant and false I sound? Why can't I be more real?" Then the thought would disappear.

The formulation is fairly obvious. The loss is being split off, obliterated, and defended against by the tremendous "manic" activity. The problem for the counselor, and it is a typical one when working with gifted individuals, is that the "manic acting out" involves much creative activity that is extremely elaborate and finely articulated with significant tracts of "reality." It is very functional and socially valuable. The task facing the therapist is how to confront the defense without throwing the baby out with the bath water—or how to find, preserve and protect the vulnerable, precious and creative baby while challenging the utility of keeping the (defensive) bath water. Fortunately, such subtle distinctions are not lost on gifted clients, and they were not lost on Don. He was able to experiment with different behaviors—for example setting a fixed time for sessions—and living with the anxiety that this released. He was able to experiment with slowing down his lifestyle without giving up the creativity of it. He was able to tolerate and work through the depressive and inadequate feelings that emerged as he both slowed down and let down. He started to connect with people—lovers and friends—more deeply, and was able to live through this more risky type of relating. Luckily, there were people to meet him in this new place, as his masks came down and he was able to resume his growth on a more authentic footing.

Don illustrates quite well the subtle, seductive quality the creations of the gifted can take on and the necessity for the counselor to both confront and respect their functions. It is easy to collude with gifted productions and not be empathic or growth facilitating to analyze them away. Janus-faced, they are both functional and defensive—serving both to illuminate and obliterate meaning. Counselors beware!

Another feature to be found in counseling the gifted that is entirely consistent with Dabrowski's theory [and slightly extends the work of Alice Miller (1981)] has to do with emotional sensitivity, which is an aspect of emotional OE. This proclivity in gifted individuals to be extremely sensitive in the area of emotions is entirely consistent with Miller's observation of the acute sensitivity gifted children develop towards the narcissistic demands of their parents. What I wish to highlight here, however, is the phenomenon of emotional amplification. Gifted individuals may have a double take on their childhood—(a) the "regular" version where the hurts and losses were average and expectable; and (b) the underground, suppressed version (their private version) which is redolent with intense feelings—feelings which do not bear the validation stamp either of themselves or their parents.

Beth

Thus, Beth, a high-achieving businesswoman with an IQ of over 130, gave two versions of her mother as a woman who never actually said anything mean (Mother A) and as an intensely attacking and hurtful harridan (Mother B). Mother B had been introjected and had taken up destructive residence in Beth's mind—oppressing the curious, lively, vigorous, energetic child and creating terribly low self-esteem. When Mother B is uncovered and revealed as the wicked and destructive internalization, the revelation is quickly undone because the client felt that she could not come up with enough objective proof of cruelty—only "small things" would come to mind. It was at this point that the counselor awareness of emotional OE or emotional amplification could be of help. It was pointed out that for Beth, a gifted child, a small cue, perhaps non-verbal, could be amplified into the crushing tirades she seemed to paradoxically remember, but not be able to document with hard evidence. At this, Beth heaved a sigh of relief and expanded upon the recurrent experience of having intense emotional responses to "small things" that her parents could not comprehend. From this, the therapist was able to form an alliance with the alienated child within and help it to give voice to its authentic experience. As this happened, of course, self-esteem and its sequelae (confidence, self enjoyment, self-acceptance) started to blossom. The OEs acted as amplifiers of Beth's experience, increasing the intensity of her response to what her parents regarded as "small things."

A similar stereoscopic vision of his family was offered by Ted (the previously mentioned 25-year-old). On the one hand his family was described as typically stable and suburban with the usual level of sibling rivalry—nothing to write home about. At other times he would describe his relationship with his brother in such a way as to evoke images of being locked in a cell with a sadistic psychopath. Again, this "sadistic psychopath" with his taunting cruelty had been internalized. As Fairbairn points out (1952) we tend to introject our bad relationships in order to gain some measure of control over them—perhaps much like management in a factory might promote a recalcitrant worker in order to co-opt that person. Once introjected, this "bad internal object" behaves as a semi-autonomous subpersonality and wreaks havoc upon the integrity of the self—creating an empty, turmoiled paralysis. As with Beth, however, once the internalization is exposed through interpretation, the awareness is quickly negated or flattened because there is no documented evidence, so to speak. What happens here is that the high level of emotional overexcitability lead to an amplification of "small" events in the life of the gifted child and adult.

As an addendum, it is important to note that when the above interpretation was offered to Ted it was met with withering scorn—scorn emanating from the introjected "bad brother" and the counselor got a taste of what Ted has to live with all the time. The client let the counselor know how it feels to have a "bad brother" living inside your mind by acting like his "bad brother" towards the counselor.

Casey

This client, a 38-year-old white female, presented with a problem of not being able to hold a job for more than a few weeks, coupled with frequent marital fights. From the point of view of OEs, I soon assessed her as having a profile similar to those described in Piechowski (1983, 1986) of gifted individuals. She evinced strong emotional ties to people and places, rendered vivid personalized images of friends and was capable of deep, intense feelings in sessions, although she was usually embarrassed with those having to do with love, caring and tenderness. These were called "stupid." From this I posited a high emotional OE. Her avid interest in thinking, theory and her insistence on logic led me to hypothesize a high intellectual OE. Similarly, a chosen field of physical education and a love for vigorous cycling and swimming led to the conclusion of a high psychomotor OE. A vividly presented enjoyment of food and talk rich in imaginative allusions led me to believe the remaining OEs were also quite high. All in all, high OEs across the board. She had the OE profile of a gifted individual (Piechowski, 1986). However, her achievements did not match this. She worked in low skill, low paid, low status jobs where she was miserable. She had not completed college and had two and one-half years to go toward a bachelor's degree.

Clearly something had happened to disrupt the full expression of her development potential. The briefest interview supported this idea. She was told she was "not wanted" as a child and existed as a "non-person" in the family for childhood and adolescence. Her talents were unrecognized and regarded as threatening by most of her family. The oases of support were thankfully present, in the form of an uncle, aunt, grandmother and teacher, but they were few and far between.

Counseling with this client involved empathic responding to her emotional states with special emphasis on "reframing" her self-perceptions in the area of her emotional responsiveness. As mentioned before, this client had intense emotional reactions to people, places and things. Frequently, however, she would describe these responses as "foolish," "dumb," or "sentimental." The counselor's empathic responsiveness implicitly validated the client's emotional overexcitabilities. In addition, the client's intellectual overexcitabilities were met with counselor comments supportive of her curiosity and love of knowledge. In conjunction with this, the client remembered with some pain being identified as a "gifted student" in junior high school and the absence of parental response to this and to her academic achievements.

An important counselor function in dealing with the emotional responsiveness was what Bion (1977) refers to as "containing," related to Winnicott's (1965) notion of "holding." In these kinds of responding, the counselor identifies the intense emotional state of the client, responds empathically to it, resonates with it, and does not "act out" to avoid the intensity of the feeling. This relates not only to the comments of the counselor, but also to the body language and behavior, all of which should provide what Langs (1974) calls a "secure frame" in which the emotions may be explored and understood. Practical ways in which the "secure frame," "containing," and a "holding environment" can be provided are by securing confidentiality, being on time in beginning and ending sessions and by avoiding interruptive or "invasive" comments or activities. The counselor also models the "containing" function by demonstrating a willingness to perceive, absorb and examine emotions.

Gradually, Casey came to regard her emotions as an asset that enriched her life and offered opportunities for contact with herself and others.

Intense emotions could be contained and reflected upon. This proved especially useful in her work with young students, as she developed a fine sensitivity for the children's emotional states and crises. She also developed deeper friendship with others, experiencing with moving poignancy feelings of love, anger, and loss. A shift took place in Casey from being possessed by emotions to having emotions.

She returned to college and started working towards graduation, becoming certified in her field and holding good grades. Her intellectual functions started to flourish. Using Dabrowski's theory, Casey could be understood as having high overexcitabilities in all five categories, but growing up in an environment that thwarted and undermined their full realization.

Using more traditional nomenclature, the features she presented would probably predispose the counselor to label Casey as a "borderline personality." A far more useful formulation, however, would be the one I have outlined, using Dabrowski's theory, in terms of overexcitabilities and the manner in which development has been thwarted.

I believe Casey exemplifies well a good proportion of cases that are labeled "borderline." The intense emotional and intellectual OE which has been thwarted creates such feelings of isolation and rage that "borderline" symptoms—intense chronic anger, feelings of abandonment, etc., emerge. If, however, the counselor reaches beyond the symptoms and contacts the underlying OEs in a validating way, the rage and abandonment dissipate in the authentic contact. These clients often appear to be a Level II of Dabrowski's theory. However, their OE profile is such, that if they are able to unlock the energy bound up in them, rapid development often ensues. Thus, they can be characterized as "Level II but passing through," i.e. on the way to Level III.

The Lure

A further aspect of work with highly talented individuals is closely related to Lacan's notion of the "Leurre" (lure or decoy [Lacan, 1977]). It is very close to my first idea regarding the subtle and enchanting quality of the character defenses of the gifted individual—only it relates more to the therapeutic interaction.

Ted, for example, would give brilliant "takes" on popular culture, television programs, pop music, news items—very entertaining, scintillating and just peppered with enough insight to convince the therapist much of the time that psychological work was being done. In actuality much of this was a "leurre"— exciting, amusing-often containing elements of truth (much as a hunting decoy might use real feather or fur) by mostly used as a means of deflecting attention from the real pain. Once this is addressed, of course, it is common for negative introjection to manifest itself, often effectively neutralizing the counselor's efforts.

Beth had had decades of therapy and was extremely verbally fluent. Long stories would flow out freely, typically without a need for interpretation. She, like many other gifted children, had learned well how to take care of her vulnerable parents and the counselor. The discourse was warm, insightful and affectively charged to all appearances, therapy was

223

taking place—but it was not—it was more along the lines of what Winnicott would term "false self therapy." Interacting with the "leurre" leads to stalemate eventually—the charming, entertaining "leurre" must be confronted if the true self is to emerge. The true self is often hidden behind the contempt and scorn of the negative internalization.

What I hope I have demonstrated and reasonably evocatively described here are four relatively common features of therapeutic work with gifted clients:

> Disorganization phenomena, which can be understood as emotional growth *in statu nascendi.*

> Valuable defensive products that bear respectful and careful confrontation.

> Emotional amplification along with amplification of all other experience; this, often combined with negative introjection, can lead gifted individuals to denigrate and question their authentic experience,

> Negation (stifling and discounting) of OEs, the "Leurre," whereby gifted clients can very effectively decoy the unaware therapist into "pseudo-therapy" leading to an empty stalemate.

The therapist can assist gifted clients in their emotional growth by introducing ideas from the Theory of Positive Disintegration. One idea that can be of help is the notion of amplification of all experience and that this results in conditions of "information overload" in potentially all of the five channels of the OEs. In the face of the added flow of amplified experience—extra intense feelings, visions, sensations, thoughts and bodily sensations—the mind has to continually reorganize and update itself-leading to an experience of chaos. An image borrowed from Bak (1996) captures the idea. Experience is analogous to grains of sand falling on a small sand pile. Amplifications of experience imply an increase in the flow of falling sand. Reorganization of the self would be analogous to avalanches of sand. Clearly the slower the flow of sand the fewer the avalanches and the more "stable" the pile. The increased flow of sand (i.e. the increased intensity of experience) leads to an increase in the frequency of the avalanches—perhaps even to the point where the pile is not so much a pile as a dynamic flow of continuous avalanches! These latter states would be analogous to positive disintegration and indeed provide a challenge of adaptation in the domain of forming a congruent, stable and positive self-concept. Dabrowski's theory, thus presented, provides an avenue towards such self-understanding.

Paradoxically, when gifted clients are presented with these ideas, they will at once accept them as accurate and at the same time resist them. This resistance is sometimes based on the notion that they are being placed in an elite group and there is a sense of shame and embarrassment at this possibility. Secondly, the insight will often activate a cruel introject (a critical parent or brother) which then tries to undo the pleasure of self-recognition. Thirdly, the act of authentic self-recognition implies taking a further step in the process of separation and individuation, both from real people ("real objects") and from internalized objects, especially the "bad introjects" and this process always evokes anxiety, depression and resistance to some degree. The counselor can empathize with these processes, to the extent that they are present, and lay the groundwork for the awe-inspiring emergence of the true self.

Because the eye gazes but can catch no

glimpse of it,

It is called elusive.

Because the ear listens but cannot hear it,

It is called the rarefied.

Because the hand feels for it but cannot find it.

It is called the infinitesimal…

These are called the shapeless shapes,

Forms without form,

Vague semblances,

Go towards them and you can see no front;

Go after them and you see no rear.

> Lao-tzu,
> *Tao The Ching* (Ch. XIV)

Chapter 8

THE HERMENEUTIC FUNCTION: F

The central thesis of this paper is that there exists, in the human mind, a hermeneutic function—a function that critically and creatively generates meanings of events—a function that creates interpretations. In addition, it is posited that psychological well being is compromised if this function's activity is hampered. Psychotherapy can be regarded as an activity that restores the fullest possible level of functioning of this hermeneutic function by exercising the play of interpretations and by uncovering the psychological phenomena, such as trauma or family or societal culture that might inhibit the activity of F, the hermeneutic function.

In my work with individuals, couples and groups I have become more and more interested in the "play" of interpretation, the mutative power of interpretation, the rules governing the generation and delivery of interpretations and notions about the validity of interpretations. Using as conceptual springboard the work of Bion encapsulated in his famous "grid" (1977), I would like to posit a hermeneutic function (F) in much the same way that Bion posited an alpha function. Bion's alpha function was a function in the mind that linked together "beta particles," minute fragments of proto-mental experience and in so linking rendered them available for thought and, ultimately, possibly for psychological work, such as dreaming, myth-making and theorizing. The hermeneutic function is a function in the mind that develops meanings for events.

There is a tremendous literature on the topic of hermeneutics. It has concerned theologians and philosophers for eons, and the last few decades a few psychologists have attempted to draw this concept into their field. This paper is a further attempt in that regard. Owing to the vast literature on the topic of hermeneutics, there is a plethora of definitions. I think all of them are more complicated than mine. Palmer (1969) gives an excellent review of four major theorists and provides a multifaceted definition that emphasizes the components of hermeneutics that "say," "explain" and "translate." Ricoeur (1970) defines hermeneutics as, "…the theory of the rules that preside over an exegesis—that is over the interpretation of a particular text, or of a group of signs that may be viewed as a text." (1970, p.8)

I will proceed as if my simple definition involves all these components—that of assertion of a meaning, that of providing an explanation, that of translating from one set of symbols and their meanings to another, and that of interpretation. Interpretation has, in addition, a predictive component that can be explicit or implicit.

Of further help to me in unraveling this knot will be another knot—the Borromean knot of Lacan (1977). This knot reminds us that our interpretations are symbolic systems that slide back and forth over other symbolic systems, that slide over (and occasionally contact, through the "call of the real," Lacan's tuché) the real. It is these interpretations that constitute "reality" which is to be differentiated from the "real." In addition, of course, there is the third loop in the knot—the "imaginary" which overlaps partially with and informs the other two loops. Imagination enriches the symbolic, but at the same time has a life of its own.

The "real" can be thought of as "things in themselves," to borrow from Kant, or as akin to the Buddhist notion of the "suchness" of things. The "real" is unapprehendable. The best we can do is construct symbolic systems that seem to capture the real. Zizek (1993) illustrates this in reference to movies, especially those of Hitchcock. He also cleverly and succinctly illustrates the notion of the "call of the real," those instances where the symbol system, in a way that is felt as uncanny, does seem to contact, albeit momentarily, the real.

Viewed from this perspective, reality can be seen as a socially constructed matrix (one is reminded of the movie, *The Matrix*) that slides over the real, in a never-ending attempt to capture its nature. The real is the referent; "reality" corresponds to Lacan's symbolic register. Disturbances in "mental health" can be understood as disturbances in the relationships between these three domains—the imaginary, the real and the symbolic. This is captured in the dream, which has elements of all three—a symbolic representation and imaginative elaboration of "daily residues" and the unconscious.

An example from geology. Take a rock sample and slice it very thin so that you have a translucent "slide." Shine a bright light through the rock slice and you see, projected on to the screen, the crystals that comprise the rock. Change the polarization of the light being projected through the rock slice; for example, project only light rays in the vertical axis and observe. A different set of crystals is seen projected on to the screen, same rock, different light. The hermeneutic function operates this way—enabling us to see things, "in a different light."

Mental health could be defined as the capacity in the individual to generate new meanings through the operation of this hermeneutic function. I posit further that the human being has a "drive" to generate meanings and if this drive is thwarted, the negative results are parallel to the thwarting of other drives or, broadly, adaptive functions. The generation of new meanings clearly would have an adaptive function in terms of the survival of the species and the individual or group; its frustration would very likely be yoked to the experiences of anxiety and depression, which could be regarded as affective warning signs to the organism that all was not well, that the task of adaptation was functioning less than optimally.

The hermeneutic function is thus linked to libido. The organism is not only driven by sexual desire or by "object-seeking" and by the many other drives posited over the years, but also by the hermeneutic drive, which in its urge to interpret and re-interpret—to constantly see things in a different light, from a different "vertex" to import Bion's felicitous term, exercises the symbolic function and constantly increases the complexity and economy of the mappings in "reality"—mappings that foster adaptation. There is perhaps a "commandment" in the human mind that reads, "Thou shalt interpret." This commandment is hard-wired and yoked to pleasure, anxiety and depression "centers" because it serves an adaptive function for individuals and groups. Violate this imperative, and symptoms, broadly defined, emerge. Of course the act of re-interpreting, especially when it concerns core attitudes or beliefs is itself disruptive, since it generates positive feedback (in the systems meaning of the term) to the previously existing set of interpretations. The new interpretation calls for a change and an excess of change also creates the affects of anxiety, depression and displeasure. This is because there is another commandment in the human mind that reads "Thou shalt keep the set of meanings relatively stable." This imperative also fosters adaptation, for to have an overly dynamic or chaotic system of meanings creates behavior that is too random and contributes to anomie.

The human being, then, has this complex task of self-regulation along the boundary region delimiting the under-exercising of the F function and the over-exercising of the F function. Much therapy can be construed as operating in this boundary zone in various roles—surveyor, stabilizer, provocateur and so on.

At the risk of redundancy, I give a further illustration—one I find useful. The matrix of social meanings can be seen as a sliding plate of a symbol system that is linked to the real—creating the sense of reality (all too often the "numbing sense of reality" that Bion (1961) describes). It is as if the real is projected onto this matrix of reality and the matrix is itself, like the real (we hypothesize) in a constant state of flux—it becomes more or less complex, it curves and deforms and re-shapes the notions of reality. Disturbances in reality-sense, such as we find in the so-called neuroses, psychoses and borderline conditions can be viewed as disturbances in this transforming function operating between the real and the symbolic. The disturbances themselves could be in many forms—overly fixed, fluid, or suffering from the problems Freud discusses in primary process thought—condensation, displacement and so on (Freud 1900). In addition, the linkages between the real and the symbolic could be dislocated, broken or shattered by the processes described in Bion's "Attacks on Linking" (1959) or by the equivalent activities of the "internal saboteur" of

Fairbairn (1952). Lacan, I believe, attributes these dislocations to a warding off of the rule of law of language and to an avoidance of the "symbolic castration" implied in following the rules of language.

The F function involves linking together thoughts and an attempt to link reality and the real. This linking, while essential to human adaptation and while pleasurable can also arouse envy and hatred in other sectors of the mind—in the psychotic parts of the personality and in the bad internalized objects. These, "hate links," for many reasons, among them the fact that links arouse affective memories of past pain and, insofar as linking is a depressive phenomenon, can arouse a destructive envy and spoiling along the lines described by Klein (1946) Rosenfeld (1965) and Lopez-Corvo (1995). Thus there is always a profound ambivalence in the individual and the group towards the hermeneutic function and its activities.

To be mentally healthy is to have a flourishing F function. What would a flourishing F function look like? It would first of all be available to the individual (and to the group and society, but that is another set of arguments). The individual would be able to generate and enjoy new interpretations of old events. The F function should not generate a paralyzing anxiety of uncertainty, but should lead to the generation of new meanings. The F function should be critical, that is, the new meanings are not just accepted wholesale but are subjected to rules of validation and exploration. The F function should be fluent, original and elaborate along the lines of Torrance's definition of creativity (1969). There should be playfulness to the F function. The F function operates, ideally in the transitional space of Winnicott (1965). This allows the F function full reign and generates sufficient affect and fantasy to enrich and modify the entire experience. The generation of affect is seen as useful not only in the "decorative" sense discussed in so many college psychology texts nor in the mnemonic sense in which affect assists memory, but in the profoundly adaptive sense outlined by Tompkins (1981) in which affect acts as an amplifier or attenuator of information, thus assisting in the adaptive processes of the organism and orienting the organism in social space. The fantasy element is essential in that it leads to a pressure for the generation of new meaning systems.

By the term *referential distance*, I mean the distance experienced by the receiver of the interpretation between the symbol system of the interpretation and the symbol system of the receiver. Client—centered therapy operates with a low referential distance. One uses concepts, language and so on that are in the client's frame of reference. For example the client says, "My birthday was a big washout" and the therapist might respond," You felt disappointed."

The client, in all likelihood is none too surprised by this response since it is not very far from his original statement. There is, however, some interpretation going on in this response. A new term, "disappointed" is introduced, and the client will likely start to interpret the event in a new way, albeit along the lines of his original interpretation. My argument is that although small, the F function is present in this type of exchange and does have its therapeutic impact. Kleinian analysis or Jungian analysis has a wider referential distance. In response to the above remark, for example, a psychodynamic therapist might pick up on the ambiguity of "birthday" and read or interpret it as "the day of my birth." Read this way, one arrives at the interpretation of "There was a feeling of disappointment on the day you were born." A dramatic interpretation indeed! Was this a baby that was not wanted? Was the mother depressed? Now, I am not arguing that this interpretation *should* be delivered; I am simply illustrating the notion of referential distance and arguing that a) it is present in all communication and b) far from being a dichotomous dimension, it is a continuous dimension and c) it is a dimension of considerable and complex therapeutic import, one that has been glossed over in the mostly simplistic "debates" between "client centered" and "psychodynamic" theorists.

Following Piaget (1976), von Bertallanffy (1968), Laszlo (1969), we can argue that the system of meanings in the individual's mind maintains a dynamic equilibrium and adjusts the input and the generation of new meanings accordingly, at times shutting down (assimilation) and at times opening up (accommodation). The referential distance utilized by a therapist (or any other communicator) can be roughly calibrated so as to match the dynamic equilibrium of the receiver. Accordingly, persons who have a primacy of assimilation over accommodation (at the given moment) would be more receptive to a low referential distance. This is found in individuals who are flooded with new experience, such as people who have experienced a recent trauma. Conversely, individuals with a primacy of accommodation over assimilation respond better to a larger referential distance. For example, a person who is a somewhat bored with their lifestyle and needs some new input might benefit from some interpretive activity that gives them a bit of a "workout" or a stretch. There are many more dimensions that come to bear on this dimension. It is far more complicated than this paragraph would make one think.

A further key and related dimension of the hermeneutic function is its rigidity. In my early studies on emptiness I found certain respondents who scored extremely high on their level of religious interest and very low on their level of experienced emptiness. It appeared to me that for these subjects their religion was a sort of prosthetic device—a very rigid and unchanging system of meanings that protected them from the experience of emptiness, and ultimately kept their minds closed and forestalled their future growth, or acted as a sort of "holding action" until further growth became possible. For these individuals, any new interpretation was shunned— shunned so quickly that even the anxiety aroused by the exercise of the hermeneutic function was not consciously experienced. Geary (1990) delineated three forms of religious experience—"means," "end" and "quest" and showed that the individual who utilized religion as an exploratory device, rather than a safe refuge, that is, the "questing" type, were significantly more prone to experiences of emptiness, as measured on the scale developed by Hazell (1984). This phenomenon is reminiscent of certain adolescents who, beset by the demands of puberty and identity formation, resist, say the examination of the deeper meanings of, say, the movie, *The Titanic*—its just a movie to them—they do not want to entertain for a moment that it might be about, say, a catastrophic derailing of mother-infant relationships. In both cases the F function has been minimized—in the dogmatic believer to act as repressive barrier to disturbing mental contents and in the adolescent of the example as a sort of "holding action" so that other developmental imperatives can be attended to. In the former cases I posit a "character armor" as described by Reich (1933) as a physical analog of the hermeneutic rigidity, there being an isomorphism between psyche and soma. In the latter cases, the character armor formed during childhood has loosened temporarily during the adolescent upheaval and this has been compensated for by rigidity in the hermeneutic system. The subtleties of providing an adequate and growth-enhancing environment given this set-up will be appreciated by anyone who has to live or work or play with adolescents.

The experience of emptiness (Hazell 1984a, 1984b, 1989) is a component of the hermeneutic function. As the old meanings are challenged by the new, there is a transitional state, an ambiguous space where the solid sense of meaning is lost. As Gramsci (1971) states, "the old has died, but the new has not yet been born and in the interregnum all sorts of morbid symptoms appear." Individuals and groups have differing capacities for tolerating the experience of emptiness. Some find it a horrid wasteland and intolerable and thus avoid the exploration of new meanings. The F function withers and symptoms appear. Others can bear it better and live through the terrible interregnum and emerge on the other side with new meanings and an enhanced capacity to generate new meanings. Therapy has its role in all this.

Therapy can be of help, not so much through the provisioning of interpretations or explanations of behavior, but more through the stimulation of the hermeneutic function. This touches on the oft-noted phenomenon of the inaccurate interpretation having a beneficial effect, so long as it is not anti-therapeutic. Anti-therapeutic comments in this framework would be comments that have the net impact of cramping the flow of hermeneutic activity. These would include comments that were grossly unempathic, over-stimulating, paradoxically stimulating (such as sadistic tickling), abandoning, or comments that were massively concrete, that is, where there is an overwhelming assumption of "realism" to import a phrase from the philosophy of science—where there is an assumption, often tacit, that the symbol system does, will, or can map, in actuality, the real. This condition leads us into the "numbing sense of reality" mentioned by Bion and we start to lose our interpretive "elbow room." The transitional space constricts, the sense of psychological safety diminishes and therapy grinds to a halt. Although, "sometimes a cigar is just a cigar," it does not bode well for the therapeutic outcome in most circumstances, if it is *always* a cigar. Under certain conditions, the inaccurate interpretation can stimulate F and have a therapeutic effect.

In this regard there is contact with the theory of "narrative therapy" and via this route, literary criticism. The client arrives and has a constructed narrative and its interpretation. Through dialogue with the therapist, new interpretations are brought forward and developed. The meaning of the narrative shifts and, along with it, the client's subjectivity, and identity. A new chapter is opened up with a new plot, characters, affects and behaviors as a result of the interpretations given to the client's original narrative. Captain Ahab arrives with a compelling obsession about a whale, and the whale is just a whale that did him wrong. Months later, the whale might be his father, his father's penis, his mother or her breast, a psychopathic bullying older brother, a lost love, or all of the above and more. Ahab is in a different world; the story has changed meaning. The point is not so much which meaning is right, but that Ahab is now actively engaging his F function. There is more to this than meets the eye. Eagleton (1983) provides us with an excellent review of various approaches to literary criticism, including the psychodynamic. The therapist, reading this book should enrich his or her capacities in the hermeneutic arena in fairly short order.

Books are sometimes burned. Persons with alternative interpretations of events or texts are also burned. While we can posit an F function, we can also posit (borrowing again from Bion) its anti-therapeutic opposite, negative F (—F). I have touched on mechanisms through which—F can operate—through the anti-libidinal ego, through attacks on linking, and while these passages referred to individuals, clearly the same processes can obtain in groups of all sorts. The "work group" described by Bion (1961) is a group in which the F function is very active and there is an active exploration of the many faces of the—F function. This atmosphere creates a feeling of profound psychological safety in which growth can occur. The group comes to resemble Bollas' *transformational object* (Bollas 1987).

Bion and others have very ably and richly described the many ways in which groups avoid such work, for example through the activity of basic assumptions such as dependency, fight-flight and pairing. The connection I am forging here is that these assumptions have the net effect of limiting F. In the dependency assumption F is limited, for example, by the wholesale swallowing of meanings provided by the guru. In the fight-flight assumption F is limited by fearful, sadistic and paranoid attacks on the dissenter. In the pairing group F is limited by having the curiosity (which is a key element of F) deflected from the total environment into a "curiosity" of a more "tabloid" nature about a mythical and magical couple. Anyone who interprets this activity is a spoilsport. Bion uses a French quotation to illustrate: "*La reponse est le malheur de la question.*" (The answer is the misfortune of the question). This captures the spirit of an open-ended curiosity—of an ever-evolving system of meanings—of an active F function.

REFERENCES AND BIBLIOGRAPHY

Allport, G., 1955, *Becoming, Basic Considerations for a Psychology of Personality,* Yale, New Haven, CT.

Allport, Vernon and Lindzey, 1960, *Study of Values,* Houghton Mifflin, Boston.

Auden, W. H. 1946, 1947, *The Age of Anxiety,* Random House, New York.

Bak, P., 1996, *How Nature Works,* New York, Springer Verlag.

Baker, C. 1969, *Ernest Hemingway: A Life Story,* Charles Scribner's Sons, New York.

Balint, M. *The Basic Fault, Therapeutic Aspects of Regression,* Brunner-Mazel, NY.

Beach, B., 1980, *Lesbian and Non-Lesbian Women: Profiles of Development and Self Actualization,* Ph.D. dissertation, University of Iowa, Iowa City.

Beckett, S. 1966, *Molloy, Malone Dies, The Unnamable, Three Novels,* Calder and Boyars, London.

_____, 1958, *Endgame,* Grove Press, New York.

249

_____, 1966, *En Attendant Godot,* Editions de Minuit, Paris.

Becker, H., 1964, *The Other Side,* Free Press, New York.

Bertallanffy, L. von. 1968, *General System Theory,* New York, Braziller.

Bion, W. 1959, "Attacks on Linking," *Second Thoughts,* London, Heinemann (1967)

_____, 1961, *Experiences in Groups,* London, Tavistock.

_____, 1977, *Seven Servants,* New York, Jason Aronson.

Bollas, C. 1987, *The Shadow of the Object,* Columbia University Press, NY.

Bowlby, J., 1980, *Loss,* Basic Books, New York.

Brofenbrenner, U., *The Challenge of Social Change to Public Policy and Development Research.* Paper presented at Society for Research in Child Development, Denver, April 2, 1975.

Bruch, H., 1973, *Eating Disorders,* Basic Books, New York.

_____, 1978, *The Golden Gage,* Harvard University Press, Cambridge, MA.

Bunyan, J., 1678, *Pilgrims Progress, Part 1,* Oxford World Classics, OUP, London, 1998.

Camus, A., 1965, *Le Mythe de Sysyphe,* Gallimard, Paris.

_____, 1942, *L'Etranger,* Gallimard, Paris.

Carlyle, T., 1838, *Sartor Resartus,* 1925, ed. Archibald MacMechan, Ginn and Co., Boston.

Cleckley, H., 1976, *The Mask of Sanity,* Mosby, St. Louis.

Colman, A.D. and Bexton, W.H. (eds) 1975, *Group Relations Reader,* Washington, DC, A.K. Rice Institute.

Colman, A.D. and Geller, W.H. (eds) 1985), *Group Relations Reader 2,* Washington, DC, A.K. Rice Institute.

Costello, C. and Comrey, A. 1967, *Scale for Measuring Depression and Anxiety,* J. Psych., 66, 303—313.

Cronbach, L., *Coefficient Alpha and the Internal Structure of Tests,* Psychometrika, 1951

Cronbach, L., *"Test Reliability," Its Meaning and Determination,* Psychometrika, 12, 1947, pp. 1-16.

Cronbach, L., Gleser, G., Nanda, H., Rajaratnam, N., *The Dependability of Behavioral Measurements,* John Wiley, New York.

Csikszentmihalyi, M. 1990, *Flow, The Psychology of Optimal Experience,* Harper and Row, New York.

Dabrowski, K. and Piechowski, M.M., 1977 *Theory of Emotional Development,* Dabor, Oceanside, New York.

Dabrowski, K., Kawczak, A., Piechowski, M., *Mental Growth through Positive Disintegration,* Gryf, London.

Dewey, J., 1938, *Experience and Education,* Macmillan, New York.

DSM IV, 1994, *Diagnostic and Statistical Manual of Mental Disorders,* Fourth Edition, American Psychiatric Association, Washington, D.C.

Dostoievsky, F., 1864, *Notes from Underground,* Epokha.

_____, 1861, *Memoirs from the House of the Dead,* Vremya, Oxford University Press, trans. Jessie Coulson, 1956, London.

Donne, J., 1624, *Devotions Upon Emergent Occasions, Meditation 17,* in Complete Poetry and

Selected Prose of John Donne, John Hayward (ed), 1929.

Durkheim, E. 1951, *Suicide,* Free Press, New York.

Dzuiban, C., Shirkey, E., *When is a Correlation Matrix Appropriate for Factor Analysis?* Psychological Bulletin, Vol. 81, No. 6, pp. 358-361.

Eagleton, T., *Literary Theory,* University of Minnesota Press, Minneapolis, MN.

Eliot, T.S., 1934, *The Wasteland: A Facsimile and Transcript of the Original Drafts,* Harcourt, Brace and Jovanovich, New York.

Erikson, E. 1963, *Childhood and Society*, Norton, New York.

_____, 1968, *Identity Youth and Crisis,* Norton, New York.

Fairbairn, W.R.D. 1952, *Psychoanalytic Studies of the Personality,* London, Routledge.

Ferenczi, S. 1955, *Final Contributions to the Problems and Methods of Psychoanalysis,* Karnac, London.

Filstead, W., 1973, *The Natural History of a Personal Problem,* unpublished doctoral dissertation,

Clive Hazell

Northwestern University, Department of Sociology.

Frankl, V., 1958, *Man's Search for Meaning,* Simon and Schuster, New York.

_____, 1965, *The Doctor and the Soul,* Simon and Schuster, New York.

_____, 1967, *Psychotherapy and Existentialism,* Simon and Schuster, New York.

_____, 1969, *The Will to Meaning,* Simon and Schuster, New York.

_____, 1975, *The Unconscious God,* Simon and Schuster, New York.

Freud, S. 1900, *The Interpretation of Dreams,* Avon, New York, 1965

Fromm, E. 1955, *The Sane Society,* Rinehart, New York.

Gage, D., Morse, P., and Piechowski, M., 1978, Measuring Levels of Emotional Development, *Genetic Psychology Monographs,* 1981; 103;129—152.

Geary, J. 1990, *Soren Kierkegaard, Religious Orientation and Christian Experience,* unpublished masters thesis, Millikin University.

Gleick, J. 1987, *Chaos,* Penguin, London.

Giovacchini, P., 1979, *Primitive Mental States,* Jason Aronson, New York.

Gorsuch, R., 1974, *Factor Analysis,* Saunders, Philadelphia, PA.

Gramsci, A., 1971 *Selections from the Prison Notebooks,* International Publishers, New York.

Grotstein, J., 1994, *Endopsychic Structure and the Cartography of the Internal World: Six Endopsychic Characters in Search of an Author,* in Fairbairn and the Origins of Object Relations Theory, Grotstein, J. and Rinsley, D. (eds) Guilford, New York.

Guntrip, H. 1969, *Schizoid Phenomena, Object Relations, and the Self,* IUP, New York.

Habermas, J., 1973, *Der Universalitatsanspruch der Hermeneutic,* in *Kultur und Kritik, M.* Suhrkamp, Frankfurt.

Hall, G., 1904, *Adolescence, D.* Appleton, New York.

Harvey, O. J., Hunt, D., and Schroder, H., 1961, *Conceptual Systems and Personality Organization,* John Wiley, New York.

Hazell, C.G., 1984a, "Experienced levels of Emptiness and Existential Concern with different levels of Emotional Development and Profile of Values," *Psychological Reports,* 1984, 55, 967-976.

_____, 1984b, "Scale for Measuring Experienced Levels of Emptiness and Existential Concern," *Journal of Psychology,* 1984, 117, 177-182.

_____, 1989, "Levels of Emotional Development with Experienced Levels of Emptiness and Existential Concern," *Psychological Reports,* 1989, 64, 835-838.

Heidegger, M., 1927, *Sein und Zeit,* Erste Halfte, Max Niemeyer Verlag, Halle.

Hemingway, E., *A Clean, Well-Lighted Place,* Scribner's Magazine, New York.

_____, 1940, *For Whom the Bell Tolls,* Charles Scribner's Sons, New York.

Hoffer, W., 1951, *Oral Aggressiveness and Ego Development,* Int. Jo. Psycho. Anal., 31; 156-160.

Jacobson, E. 1964, *The Self and the Object World,* International Universities Press, New York.

Joreskog, K., and Marielle van Thillo, "New Rapid Algorithms for Factor Analysis by Unweighted Least Squares, Generalized Least Squares and Maximum Likelihood," *Educational Testing Service, Research Bulletin,* 71-5.

Kafka, F., 1926, *Das Schloss,* Kurt Wolff Verlag, Munchen.

_____, 1925, *Der Prozess,* Verlag Die Schmeide, Berlin.

_____, 1927, *Amerika,* Kurt Wolff Verlag, Munchen.

Kaiser, H., Caffrey, J., "Alpha Factor Analysis," *Psychometrika, Vol.* 30, pp. 1-14, 1965.

Keniston, K., 1960, *The Uncommitted,* Delta, New York.

Kernberg, O., 1975, *Borderline Conditions and Pathological Narcissism,* New York, Jason Aronson.

_____, 1976, *Object Relations Theory and Clinical Psychoanalysis,* New York, Jason Aronson.

Klein, M. 1935/1964, "A Contribution to the Psychogenesis of Manic-Depressive States," *Contributions to Psychoanalysis.* McGraw Hill, New York.

_____, 1946, "Notes on Some Schizoid Mechanisms," in *Writings of Melanie Klein, Volume 3, Envy and Gratitude and Other Works,* Hogarth Press, London.

Koestler, A., 1945, *Darkness at Noon,* Macmillan, New York.

Kohut, H. 1971, *The Analysis of the Self,* I.U.P., New York.

_____, 1977, *The Restoration of the Self,* I.U.P., New York.

Kierkegaard, S., 1843, *Fear and Trembling,* Princeton University Press, 1954.

_____, 1846, *Two Ages,* Princeton University Press, 1978.

_____, 1849, *The Sickness Unto Death,* Princeton University Press, 1968.

Kohlberg, L., 1981, *Essays on Moral Development,* Harper and Row, San Francisco, CA.

Lacan, J. 1977, *Ecrits, A Selection,* Norton, New York.

Laing, R. 1969, *The Divided Self,* Pantheon, New York.

Langer, S., 1967-72, *Mind: An Essay in Human Feeling,* Johns Hopkins Press, Baltimore, MD.

Langs, R. 1978, *The Listening Process,* Jason Aronson, New York.

Laszlo, E., 1969, *System, Structure, and Experience,* Gordon and Breach, New York.

Lao-tsu, *Tao Teh Ching,* (trans.   Aleister Crowley), 1976, Askin Pubs., London.

Levinson, D., 1978, *The Seasons of a Man's Life,* Knopf, New York.

Loevinger, J., 1976, *Ego Development,* Jossey Bass, San Francisco, CA.

Lopez-Corvo, R., 1995, *Self Envy,* Aronson, New York.

Lowen, A., 1972, *Depression and the Body,* Penguin, New York.

Lysy, K., Piechowski, M., *An Empirical Study of Personal Growth: Jungian and Dabrowskian Measures* (in preparation).

Maddi, S., "The Existential Neurosis," *Journal of Abnormal Psychology,* 1967, 72, 311-325.

Mahler, M. 1975, *The Psychological Birth of the Human Infant,* Basic Books, New York.

Menzies-Lyth, I., 1960, *A Case Study in the Functioning of Social Systems as a Defense Against Anxiety,* Human Relations, 13: 95-121.

Mann, T., 1930, *Mario and the Magician,* (Trans. H. T. Lowe-Porter) M. Secker, London.

Marradi, A., 1981, "Factor Analysis as an Aid in the Formation and Refinement of Empirically Useful Concepts," in *Factor Analysis and Measurement in Sociological Research,* eds. Jackson, D., and Borgatta, E., Sage Publications, London.

Maslow, A., 1968, *Toward a Psychology of Being,* Van Nostrand, Princeton.

Masterson, J., 1972, *The Treatment of the Borderline Adolescent,* Wiley, New York.

May, R., 1950, *The Meaning of Anxiety,* Simon and Schuster, New York.

_____, 1953, *Man's Search for Himself,* Signet, Norton, New York.

Miller, A., 1981, *Prisoners of Childhood,* Basic Books, New York.

Musil, R., 1930, *The Man Without Qualities,* 1965, Capricorn, New York.

Ogden, T. 1983, "The Concept of Internal Object Relations," in *Fairbairn and the Origins of Object Relations,* eds. Grotstein, J. and Rinsley, D., Guilford, New York (1994)

Offer, D., Ostrov, E., and Howard, K., 1981, *The Adolescent: A Psychological Self Portrait,* Basic Books, New York.

Ogburn, M. K., 1976, *Differentiating Guilt According to Theory of Positive Disintegration,* Unpublished doctoral Dissertation, University of Wisconsin-Madison, Counseling and Guidance.

Pascal, B., 1670, *Pensees,* 1965, Armand Colin, Paris.

Perls, F., 1965, *Gestalt Therapy Verbatim,* Real People Press, Lafayette, CA.

_____, 1973, *The Gestalt Approach and Eyewitness to Therapy*, Bantam, New York.

Piaget, J. 1976, *Piaget Sampler,* ed. Sarah Campbell, Wiley, New York.

Piechowski, M., Silverman, L., Cunningham, K., Falk, R., *A Comparison of Intellectually Gifted and Artists on Five Dimensions of Mental Functioning,* Paper Presented at the American Educational Research Association Annual Meeting, March 1982, New York.

Piontelli, A. 1992, *From Fetus to Child,* Routledge, London.

Reich, W. 1933, *Character Analysis,* Orgone Institute Press, New York.

Rice, A.K., 1965, *Learning for Leadership,* Tavistock, London.

Ricoeur, P., 1970, *Freud and Philosophy: An Essay on Interpretation,* Yale, New Haven, CT.

Robert, J., Piechowski, M., 1980, "Two Types of Emotional and Intellectual Overexcitability: Conserving and Transforming," *Theory of Positive Disintegration Proceedings of the Third International Conference,* ed. Norbert John Duda, 1981, University of Miami, FL.

Rogers, C. 1961, *On Becoming a Person,* Houghton Mifflin, Boston, MA.

Rosenfeld, H., 1965, *Psychotic States,* Hogarth, London.

Rummel, R., 1970, *Applied Factor Analysis,* Northwestern University Press, Evanston, IL.

Sartre, J.P., 1956, *Being and Nothingness,* Philosophical Library, New York.

_____, 1938, *La Nausee,* Gallimard, Paris.

Schactel, E., 1959, *Metamorphosis,* Basic Books, New York.

Schact, R., 1970, *Alienation,* Anchor, New York.

Searles, H., 1979, *Countertransference,* IUP, New York.

Spitz, R., 1965, *The First Year of Life,* IUP, New York.

Spranger, E., 1928, *Types of Men, the Psychology and Ethics of Personality,* Trans by Paul Pigors, Niemeyer Verlag, (reprinted by) Johnson Reprint Co., New York, 1966.

Streng, F., 1967, *Emptiness; a Study in Religious Meaning,* Abingdon Press, Nashville, TN.

Sullivan, H. S., 1953, *Interpersonal Theory of Psychiatry,* Norton, New York.

Suzuki, D., 1956, *Zen Buddhism,* Anchor, New York.

Tillich, P., 1952, *The Courage to Be,* Yale University Press.

Tolstoy, L., 1868, *War and Peace,* Oxford University Press, London, 1930.

Tompkins, S., 1981, "Affect as Amplification, Some Modifications in Theory." In Plutchik, R., and Kerrerman, H., (eds) *Emotion, Theory, Research and Experience. Vol 1: Theories of Emotion.* New York, Academic Press.

Torrance, E.P., 1969, *Creativity,* Adapt Press, Sioux Falls, ND.

Tustin, F., 1972, *Autism and Childhood Psychoses,* Hogarth, London.

Vonnegut, K., 1976, *Slapstick,* Delacorte Press, New York.

Warnock, M., 1965, *The Philosophy of Sartre,* Hutchinson, London.

Winnicott, D. W., 1960, "Ego Distortion in Terms of True and False Self," in *The Maturational Processes and the Facilitating Environment,* pp 140-152, Hogarth, London.

_____, 1964, *The Child, The Family, and the Outside World,* Pelican, New York.

_____, 1965a, *The Maturational Processes and the Facilitating Environment,* IUP, New York.

_____, 1965b, *The Family and Individual Development,* Tavistock Publications, London.

_____, 1971a, *Therapeutic Consultations in Child Psychiatry,* Hogarth, London.

_____, 1971b, *Playing and Reality,* Basic Books, New York.

Yalom, I., 1980, *Existential Psychotherapy,* Basic Books, New York.

Yeats, W. B., 1989, "The Second Coming" in *Collected Poems of W. B. Yeats,* Finneran, R.J. (ed), Macmillan, New York.

Zizek, S., 1993, *Looking Awry,* MIT, Cambridge, MA.

ABOUT THE AUTHOR

Clive Hazell has a private practice in counseling and consulting in Chicago, Illinois, where he has lived for over thirty years. He received a PhD from Northwestern University and teaches at The Illinois School of Professional Psychology, The School of the Art Institute of Chicago, and DeVry University. His long-standing interest in emptiness was stimulated by encounters with Zen while studying undergraduate geography at Reading University, England. Other interests include guitar, songwriting, long distance running, bird watching and rugby.

Printed in the United States
16140LVS00001B/82-99